Inspector of Irish Fisheries

Inspectors of Irish Fisheries report, 1878

Inspector of Irish Fisheries

Inspectors of Irish Fisheries report, 1878

ISBN/EAN: 9783741104534

Manufactured in Europe, USA, Canada, Australia, Japa

Cover: Foto ©ninafisch / pixelio.de

Manufactured and distributed by brebook publishing software
(www.brebook.com)

Inspector of Irish Fisheries

Inspectors of Irish Fisheries report, 1878

REPORT

OF THE

INSPECTORS OF IRISH FISHERIES

ON THE

SEA AND INLAND FISHERIES OF IRELAND,

FOR

1878.

Presented to both Houses of Parliament by Command of Her Majesty.

DUBLIN:
PRINTED BY ALEXANDER THOM, 87 & 88, ABBEY-STREET,
PRINTER TO THE QUEEN'S MOST EXCELLENT MAJESTY.
FOR HER MAJESTY'S STATIONERY OFFICE.

1879.

[C.—2333.] *Price 9½d.*

CONTENTS.

REPORT

OF THE

INSPECTORS OF IRISH FISHERIES

ON THE

SEA AND INLAND FISHERIES OF IRELAND, FOR 1878.

TO HIS GRACE JOHN WINSTON, DUKE OF MARLBOROUGH, K.G.,
&c., &c., &c.

LORD LIEUTENANT-GENERAL AND GENERAL GOVERNOR OF IRELAND.

MAY IT PLEASE YOUR GRACE,

We have the honour, in conformity with the 112th sec. of the 5th & 6th Vic., cap. 106, to submit our Report for the year 1878, being the tenth since the Sea and Inland Fisheries of Ireland have been placed under the superintendence of this Department.

SEA FISHERIES.

According to the returns received from the Coast Guard, the number of vessels engaged in fishing for sale in 1878 was 5,759, the number of men so engaged 19,920, and boys 806.

Of the above, 1,525 vessels were solely engaged in fishing, with crews amounting to 6,319, men and boys. The remainder, 4,234 vessels, with 14,407 men and boys, were only partially so engaged.

The foregoing shows an increase of 377 vessels, and 333 men and boys employed in the Sea Fisheries of Ireland, as compared with the returns for 1877.

Although every effort has been made to secure accuracy in the returns of boats and persons engaged in the fisheries, we cannot say that this has yet been attained, but it is believed, that, on the whole, the present return is more correct than those hitherto issued.

It may appear strange that it should be difficult to secure accuracy in such returns, but when it is remembered, that the subordinate officers of Coast Guards in charge of the different stations, who have to prepare these returns, are frequently changed, the great extent of many of their Guards, and the reluctance shown by the fishermen in some parts of the coast to give information, the difficulty will be more easily understood.

The following is an extract from the instructions issued by this Department for the year 1878, for the guidance of officers in performing this duty :—

"1. Every boat engaged in sea fishing where any portion of the fish is sold should be included in this Return, *whether Registered or Unregistered.*

"2. No vessel or boat should be returned as a fishing craft unless some portion of the fish taken is sold.

"3. Return only as fishermen persons employed in sea fishing boats that capture for purpose of sale.

"4. As fishermen frequently fish in different boats, according to the season, care should be taken that the names of such men are shown only in one place.

"5. Every effort should be made to enforce the Registry of all Boats used for Fishing, when any part of the fish is sold.—Boats engaged only in Salmon Fishing need not be so registered.

"As many fishermen entertain groundless objections to registering, it should be explained to them that they incur no liability or expense by registration, and are liable to a penalty for neglecting it."

Notwithstanding these instructions, which it is considered should be sufficient to ensure correctness and uniformity, it is found that some of the Officers take different views of what is required ; hence the great difficulty above referred to.

We feel bound again to bring under Your Grace's notice the fact that the usefulness of this Department would be very largely increased, if we had attached to it a properly equipped vessel, which would enable us, not only to visit islands situated off the coast, but, to carry out experiments in different modes of fishing, and for the discovery of new fishing grounds.

It has often been alleged that, off the west coast, very large and productive banks, which abound with valuable fish, are to be found, and it is believed that different kinds of fish, which are not generally looked for, and but little known in this country, frequent parts of our coasts.

Such matters as these require to be thoroughly investigated, and we respectfully submit that the advantages, which it is believed would result to the country from such investigations, would far outweigh the cost of providing this Department with the means of making them.

As usual, the conduct of the fishermen around the coast is reported as very satisfactory.

Galway Bay.

The removal of the restrictions against trawling in certain parts of Galway Bay, by our Bye-law, dated 31st August, 1877, and which was confirmed and came into force on the 11th February, 1878, has been found beneficial in securing a large capture of fish by the trawlers, whilst at the same time the line fishermen have also had a very successful season.

It was anticipated by many persons that the removal of the restrictions might lead to considerable opposition and resistance on the part of some of the parties interested; but, happily, up to the present no serious unpleasantness has resulted.

Some complaints have been received of the trawlers having damaged and carried away portions of the lines of some of the local fishermen. These reports have been rather exaggerated, but it is hoped that by the exercise of greater caution on the part of the trawlers, no future grounds of complaint will arise.

Trawling on the East Coast.

In our last Annual Report mention was made of our intention to hold inquiries to ascertain whether or not it would be desirable to make some change in the regulations respecting trawling along portions of the east coast.

Up to the present, the pressure of our other duties has prevented our being able to hold these inquiries, but we trust in a short time to have the subject investigated, especially as representations have been made to us in the interest of some of the trawl fishermen.

Oyster Fisheries.

Nothing especially deserving attention has occured in respect of the oyster fisheries.

There was a fair fall of spat in some localities, but it was by no means general.

Seven new licences to plant oysters have been granted, and four withdrawn.

The Arklow fishery produced 7,325 barrels. During the year the price realized averaged £1 per barrel.

The French oysters, laid down in the private beds, have in some cases, thriven well, but it cannot be said that they have proved quite successful, generally. Most of these were imported from Arcachon.

In his Report on the Oyster Fisheries of France, dated 28th February, 1878, Major Hayes, at pages 22 and 23, remarks that along the French coast he found "in proceed-"ing south the invariable opinion at the different places to be much in favour of the "oysters imported from the district of Auray; they were said to be hardier, that they "thrive better, and that the loss in transport is less than those from Arcachon."

In only one place in Ireland have oysters been imported from Auray, viz., at Omeath, Carlingford Lough, by C. O. Woodhouse, esq., and his experience fully bears out the opinions of the French cultivators. It is understood that the loss in those imported by him has not amounted to three per cent.; they have thriven well; and have become since they were laid down more like the native Irish oyster than any brought from the Arcachon district.

We are strongly of opinion that it would be to the advantage of oyster culturists generally, to import from the Auray or Vannes districts instead of Arcachon. It should be remembered that the two former places are somewhere about 150 or 160 miles further north than the latter; the temperature consequently is not nearly so high, and thus does not differ in so great a degree from our own climate.

Hitherto, difficulties in obtaining direct transit from Auray or Vannes to Ireland have been greater than from Arcachon, but these can be surmounted; and it is understood that through rates may be obtained to Dublin or Greenore by communicating with the authorities of the London and North Western Railway Company.

The Herring Fisheries.

The quantity of Herrings captured at nine places from which we are enabled to procure reliable statistics amounted to 169,603 mease. The average price per mease at which they were sold was £1 2*s.* 9*d.*, producing in the aggregate a sum of £220,278 as compared with 284,424 mease, averaging £1 5*s.* 9*d.* per mease, taken in 1877.

Very large quantities are taken along the western coast, but it is impossible to obtain reliable returns of the capture.

Herring Fishery, 1878.

—	Boats employed and highest number on any one day.				Total Capture.	Average Price.	Value.
	English.	Scotch	Irish	Manx			
					Mease.	£ s. d.	£
Howth, between 24th May and 7th Dec., 1878,	210	215	330	210	68,060	1 3 6	86,694
Arklow, between 9th June and 15th Dec, 1878,	–	–	91	–	6,359	0 16 8	5,285
Kinsale, between 20th April and 21st Dec, 1878,	–	20	29	8	1,372	1 17 5	2,568
Greenore, between 4th June and 27th Nov., 1878,	–	5	45	11	46,754	1 3 8	55,155
Ardglass, between 25th May and 7th Dec., 1878,	40	152	79	37	58,335	1 1 10	63,830
Omeath and Warrenpoint, between 4th June and 19th Oct., 1878,	–	15	50	105	435	1 4 0	546
Kilkeel, between 1st June and 1st Nov., 1878,	200	48	75	–	1,300	1 5 0	1,625
Annalong,	–	–	35	–	9,000	1 0 0	9,000
Courtown,	–	–	35	–	1,968	0 16 0	1,574
					193,603	1 2 9	220,278

It will be seen that the number of Irish boats employed in the herring fishery has largely increased since 1877.

It may be well to refer to a mistaken idea which prevails largely in this country on the subject of the herring fishery, with regard to the alleged disadvantages the Irish fishery labours under in not having an established government brand for cured herrings, as in Scotland.

In the year 1876 we received instructions from the Chief Secretary to inquire into and report for the information of his Grace the Lord Lieutenant our opinion upon the advisability of extending to Ireland the Scotch system of branding herrings, and also whether any practical benefit would really be derived from such extension, having regard to the circumstances of the Irish herring fishery trade.

It should be borne in mind, that, at the great centres of the herring fishery in Ireland, the fish are sold by auction directly after being caught, and are paid for on the spot; and the great bulk is immediately dispatched to England by special steamers employed for the purpose.

The following is an extract from the unanimous report made by our Board, dated January, 1877 :—

"One of our Board (Mr. Brady), proceeded to Scotland and investigated the details connected with the Scotch herring fisheries, and the branding system pursued in certain places there. A copy of his report is annexed." (Copy sent with report).

"Inquiries were also held at the principal herring fishery stations in Ireland by Mr. Blake and Major Hayes, and we investigated the subject from time to time at other places, as opportunity offered.

"After a very careful consideration of the question on every point, we have to report that we are unable to recommend that the branding system should be extended to this country, and in this we are mainly influenced by the following reasons :—

"1st. Although it has from time to time been argued that the introduction of the brand would lead to a further development of the herring fisheries in Ireland, we have been unable to find that any *bona fide* desire for it exists amongst the Irish fishermen or curers.

"2nd. It appears that in Scotland, where the fish are cured for the foreign markets, the price received by the fishermen is about 22*s* per cran of 960 herrings; whereas in Ireland, sold by auction immediately after being caught, they have realized much higher prices to the captors, as will be seen by the following average prices of the last four years. The Irish herrings realized—

"In 1873—£1 5*s.* per mease of 630—equal to about £1 10*s.* 0*d.* per cran.

" 1874—Irish herrings sold at 18*s.* 9*d.* per mease—equal to £1 7*s.* 4½*d.* per cran.

" 1875—Irish herrings sold at £1 1*s.* 9*d.* per mease—equal to about £1 13*s.* 7½*d.* per cran.

" 1876—Irish herrings sold at £1 6*s.* per mease—equal to £1 19*s.* per cran.

"These figures show that under present circumstances the Irish fishermen realize much higher prices than those obtained in Scotland.

"3rd. Any herrings cured at present in Ireland, as a matter of fact, sell at higher prices than can be obtained for the highest brand of Scotch herrings. Therefore, in our opinion, the extension to Ireland of the Scotch branding system would not be advisable, and we consider that no material benefit would really be derived from such extension, having regard to the circumstances of the Irish fishery trade."

The Mackerel Fishery.

The Kinsale fishery for 1878 was not so satisfactory as the season 1877, the gross capture, as taken from the returns, amounting only to 92,626 boxes of six score each, as compared with 114,362 boxes in the previous year.

The prices realized varied from 90*s.*, the highest, to 5*s.*, the lowest, per box, producing in the aggregate a sum of £97,788 8*s.* 6*d.*, being an average of a little over 21*s.* per box.

It is believed that the season would have been a very successful one but for the destructive gale which set in on the 26th March, and which resulted in placing about half the fleet *hors de combat*.

Large numbers of boats lost their entire trains of nets, and on the 3rd April it was estimated that not more than one third of the fleet was able to fish—many boats with only half trains. Seventy or eighty boats had to return home to procure new trains, whilst many others were engaged in repairing and clearing what little they had left.

It is but seldom that any loss of life occurs amongst the fleet attending the mackerel fishery, but on the present occasion we regret to say that eleven men were lost—viz., 7 men, the entire crew of the *Somerset*, No. 49, of Peel, which foundered with all hands; two men of the *Mary Lily*, of Port St. Mary, and two men from the *Dolly Varden*, of Arklow; altogether, eleven men.

One boat owner is believed to have lost over £2,000 in consequence of the gale, and the total loss is estimated at between twenty-five and thirty thousand pounds.

A great part of the month of April was thus lost to a large portion of the fleet, which fully accounts for the diminished capture.

In last year's Report we referred to the great desirability of the port of Kinsale being provided with the usual storm signals, and in February, 1877, we made a representation on the subject to the authorities. After a lengthened correspondence with various departments, the Meteorological Department of the Board of Trade consented to grant the use of the storm signals, and to cause notices of any serious atmospheric disturbance to be forwarded from time to time.

The Admiralty also having consented to the signals being placed in charge of the chief officer of Coast Guard at Summer Cove, Kinsale, and the Harbour Commissioners having provided certain necessary gear in the way of ropes and blocks, the signals were duly established since June last.

We trust that in the coming season, and for the future, this will be a means of guarding against a repetition of the serious catastrophes of 1876–7.

During the season there were 265 English and Manx boats, 20 Scotch, and 190 Irish attending the mackerel fishery, being a further increase of Irish boats since last year of 18, and since 1871 of 90, thus showing year by year that more interest is being exhibited in Ireland in developing this important fishery.

During the season nine vessels arrived from Norway laden with ice, their gross tonnage amounting to 5,707 tons. The ice was stored at Kinsale in twenty-one vessels used as hulks, their tonnage amounting to 2,103 tons.

Eight steamers and four Jersey cutters were constantly employed, besides occasional tug-boats from Queenstown, conveying the fish to England.

In addition to our own fleet, there were 107 French luggers employed at the fishery, and it is believed many of them filled up two or three times, returning each time to the fishing ground after taking their cargoes to France.

Complaints were made of some of the French crews interfering with the nets of our boats; but, as far as could be ascertained, after due inquiry, the complaints were unfounded.

A certain amount of jealousy prevails against foreigners coming on the fishing ground, more especially amongst the Manx fishermen; and we fear this will always continue: but as a rule the foreign boats fish far out to sea, to the westward, and generally keep clear of our boats.

It might be worth the attention of parties engaged in the mackerel fishing, to consider whether in some things they might not with advantage take a lesson from the Frenchmen. The French boats are larger than ours, their nets much longer, and many of them have on board a small engine with which to haul their nets and to raise their masts. In a few cases they are provided with a small screw propeller, which can be connected with the engine, when required, to move to or from the fishing ground in adverse winds or calms, thus saving much time—a matter of importance, in a season, which only lasts about three months.

Mackerel in considerable quantities are captured off many other parts of the coasts; but, as conveyance to the English markets is difficult, they are generally consumed locally.

During March and April the prices for mackerel ranged high, but at the end of April and during May they fell considerably. A few boats then took out their herring nets, and were fairly successful, the average take per boat, per week, being about £37. In some cases they were more fortunate, their capture amounting in the week to as much as £55 per boat. The herring fishing was done principally by Scotch and Irish boats.

The Pilchard Fishery.

Pilchards in considerable shoals appeared as usual off many parts of the coasts of Cork and Kerry, especially the former; and if proper arrangements were made for their capture and to cure them for foreign markets, it is believed the enterprise would prove remunerative.

As alluded to in our last Report, a small company was formed at Baltimore, county Cork, with the object of taking and curing these fish. It is understood that they succeeded in curing between three and four hundred hogsheads, the greater part of these having been purchased from the local fishermen. From some cause which has not been explained to us, the nets of the company were not as successful as they might have been, their capture not much exceeding one-fourth of what was cured.

We entertain little doubt that fisheries of this kind properly worked, with the necessary appliances for curing, would pay satisfactorily in some parts of the coast.

Piers and Harbours.

The following, which has been received from the Commissioners of Public Works, will show what progress has been made since our Report of last year:—

1. Giles'-quay, county Louth,	Completed and handed over to county. Total expenditure in the construction, £9,358 12s. 6d.
2. Poul-Hurrin, Gortalia, county Donegal,	Engineer's examination not yet made.
3. Malinbeg, county Donegal,	Do. do.
4. Port-Oriel, Clogher Head,	Completed. Additional works if undertaken can be completed this season.
5. Tawney, county Donegal,	Engineer's examination not yet made.
6. Muckross, county Donegal,	Do. do.
7. Ballymaggart, county Donegal,	Do. do.
8. Scattery Island, county Clare,	Engineer's estimate £700. Communicated to memorialists—no reply.
9. Bournapeaka, Ballyvaughan, county Clare,	Will be completed early this year.
10. Smeerogue or Poolally, county Galway,	Engineer's examination not yet made.
11. Mulranny, county Mayo,	Engineer's estimate sent to memorialists. Awaits presentment and contribution.
12. Scilly, Kinsale, county Cork,	Inquiry as to the best site pending.
13. Burton Port, county Donegal,	Engineer's estimate sent to memorialists, who propose a smaller sum.
14. North Harbour, or Kearn's Port, Cape Clear, county Cork,	In progress. Will be completed within next year.
15. Ardglass, county Down,	In progress. Contractor to complete work by 1st December, 1880.
16. Cheekpoint, county Waterford,	Not yet reported on by Engineer.

It is to be regretted that the decision of the Treasury not to grant Loans in aid of Fishery Piers, until the Harbours of Ardglass and Arklow have been completed, remains still in force. The advantage to the country generally of providing safe and convenient shelter for fishing boats would in our opinion be of such importance in developing the fisheries around our coasts as ought to secure that every encouragement should be given to provide them wherever required.

The important work now being carried on at Ardglass Harbour, which we have recently inspected, we have little doubt will, when completed, give a great impetus to the east coast herring fishery, not only by tending to increase the number of fishing vessels but by enabling the fishermen to continue their fishing to a later period in each season than hitherto.

The want of shelter in the harbour, in consequence of the partial destruction of the old pier, rendered it so unsafe in certain winds, which prevail late in the season, that the herring fleet have generally to take their departure at an earlier period than they would otherwise have done.

It is hoped that in carrying out this most important work the existence of a very dangerous ledge of rocks almost in the centre of the harbour has not been overlooked. The ledge alluded to, called the "Churn Rock," has long been regarded with dread by the fishermen, and several wrecks have occurred upon it—its removal, during the progress of the present work, could be easily accomplished, and would largely increase the harbour accommodation, which is much needed; unless this is done the harbour will always be insufficient for the requirements of the herring fishing fleet.

Reproductive Loan Fund.

Reports will be found from the inspectors, with regard to the administration of this fund in their respective divisions.

The amount available for 1878 was £6,741. The sum applied for, £11,802 14s., embracing 557 applications and comprising 945 persons.

300 loans comprising 457 persons for £5,588 10s. were recommended. 21 loans were cancelled or not perfected for £308, so that £5,187 10s. was actually issued on 279 loans up to date of this Report.

In the county Limerick £625 available, but only one application was received.

In county Sligo £267 was issued out of £449 available, and in the county Kerry £2,304 was taken up out of £2,450 available. As will be seen in the Appendix, with the exception of the counties of Leitrim and Limerick, the amount applied for far exceeded the amount available.

In the four years since the passing of the Irish Reproductive Loan Fund Act, up to 31st December, 1878, 1,078 loans for a total sum of £19,352 have been made, and up to that date repayments have been received amounting to £10,776 3s. 6d.

The amount overdue up to the present time is £228 14s. 4d.—much of this will be recovered—so that the losses by defaulters will, as far as we can at present form an estimate, be more than provided for by the rate of interest (2½ per cent.) charged, and thus the original fund will be preserved intact.

Considering the bad harvest of 1878, and the bad fishing season in many parts of the country, we cannot but consider that the results, up to the present, are most satisfactory.

STATE OF THE SEA FISHERIES.

Dublin Division.

From Howth to Greystones, both Stations inclusive.

According to the Coast Guard Returns there are in this division 193 fishing craft, with 723 men and 104 boys employed in same, as compared with 199 vessels and boats, with 555 men and 64 boys, in 1877.

Trawling, long and hand lines, and draft nets are the means of capture.

Large shoals of mackerel appeared off Greystones in August and September, for which adequate means of capture existed. Herrings, cod, plaice, soles, turbot, whiting, and other fish are caught.

The only lobster and crab fishing in this district is at Bray Head, and between Dalkey and Bullock. About 3 dozen lobsters and 5 dozen crabs a week during the season were taken here, but the size was small.

The conduct of the fishermen throughout the district was good.

No part of the division is unguarded.

Oyster Fisheries.

From the oyster beds of Clontarf about £280 worth of oysters were sold during the year. The Sutton oyster beds, from stock laid down in 1877, at a cost of £2,007, sent to the market 248,000 large oysters and 245,000 small ones, realizing altogether £2,852 1s. 6d.

Arklow Division.

From the Breaches, County Wicklow, North, to the Sluices, near Cahore, County Wexford, South, a length of 56½ miles.

No portion of this division unguarded.

The Coastguard Returns show as employed in the fisheries during 1878, 345 vessels, 1,347 men, and 67 boys, which, as compared with our report of last year, would give an apparent increase of 3 vessels, but a decrease of 284 men and an increase of 58 boys.

Of the boats, 9 were of the first class, 281 second, and 55 of the third.

The fish principally taken are herrings, cod, oysters, and trawl fish. Mode of fishing, nets, lines, dredges, and trawls.

There were 7,825 barrels of oysters taken from the banks. Average price per barrel 20s., realizing £7,825.

From one ground it is reported that the spatting was much the same as in 1877. In the Arklow ground the report is unfavourable.

Shoals of mackerel appeared about a quarter of a mile from the shore in September between Ardmore and Mizen Head, a little south of Wicklow.

It is understood that although nothing definite has, we believe, been decided upon about the projected improvements to Arklow Harbour, yet, that negociations are going on on the subject, and in the interests of the fisheries it is to be hoped that some decision may be speedily arrived at.

The conduct of the fishermen was good.

Wexford Division.

From the Sluices near Cahore to Bannow Bay.

The Harbour of Wexford, from Rosslare to Raven Point, is unguarded, being under the control of the Customs Authorities.

In this division there are 166 boats, 612 men, and 5 boys engaged in sea-fishing. Of these 14 are first class boats, 133 second, and 19 third.

Solely engaged in fishing, 60 boats, 147 men, and 4 boys; partially, 106 boats, 465 men, and 1 boy. Fish generally captured—Herrings, mackerel, cod, bream, conger, pollock, &c.

The modes of fishing are drift and trawl nets, hand and long lines.

Shoals of mackerel and herrings appeared off the coast between August and November.

Lobsters and crabs of fine quality were captured in great numbers around the Saltee Islands, and generally between this and the entrance of Wexford Harbour considerable numbers were taken.

The fishermen are reported as well behaved. Nothing especially deserving note has occurred during the year.

Waterford Division.

From East Bank of Bannow Ferry to Ballyvoile Head, north of Dungarvan Harbour.

This division extends along the coast for a distance of 62½ miles, all of which is guarded; but in the estuaries the following portions are unguarded :—

From Oyster Point to Wellington Bridge, 5 miles; from Ballyhack to Fisherstown, 8 miles; from Glass House to Rochestown, 7 miles; from Churchpoint to Blackrock, 10 miles; total 30 miles.

In the division there are 137 boats, 356 men, and 18 boys employed in the sea fisheries—13 first class boats, 100 second class, and 24 third class.

Of the above there are solely engaged in fishing, 20 boats, 49 men, 11 boys; partially so engaged, 117 boats, 307 men, 7 boys.

The fish principally taken are plaice, soles, turbot, brill, bream, cod, hake, ling, mackerel, whiting, and sprats, and occasionally herrings in large quantities.

The modes of fishing are trawling, seines, long-lines, hand-lines, &c.

There has been an unusually good supply of mackerel and sprats, and they are reported to have remained later than usual off the west end of the division.

The supply of lobsters and crabs is stated to have been good.

Oysters are said to be decreasing.

It is reported that off Bonmahon more mackerel, bream, cod, whiting, and mackerel were seen, but the take was not large owing to the want of proper gear for their capture.

The fishermen are reported to have been orderly and well conducted.

Youghal Division.

From Ballyvoile Head, near Dungarvan, to Ballycottin; a distance of 56½ miles.

Unguarded :—From Tullacort Point to Ballyvoile Bridge, two miles; from Mine Head, East, to Corrin River, West, six and three-quarter miles; from Goat Island to Ferry Point, five miles; from Glanwilliam to Ballycrivane, five miles; total, 18¾ miles.

The Coast Guard returns show as engaged in the sea fisheries 128 boats, 610 men, 6 boys, viz. :—9 first-class boats, 79 second-class, and 40 third-class. Of these 33 boats, 217 men, and 5 boys are shown as solely engaged in fishing, and 95 boats, 393 men, and 1 boy only partially so engaged.

Hake, cod, ling, plaice, soles, mackerel, bream, whiting, and large quantities of sprats were captured.

Large shoals of mackerel, pilchards, and sprats in July, August, and September.

Inadequate means for the capture of mackerel.

Large quantities of lobsters and crabs were taken in the season.

The fishermen reported as very orderly.

Queenstown Division.

From Garryroe, in Ballycottin Bay, West, to Lane's Cottages, Ringabella Point, East. Length of coast, 110 miles.

Unguarded portion of division :—All the estuary of Cork Harbour, from and including Queenstown to the City of Cork.

The returns show that 209 boats, 564 men, and 55 boys were engaged in the sea-fisheries in 1878, viz. :—7 first-class boats, 110 second-class, and 92 third-class. Of these 98 boats, 303 men, 29 boys were solely engaged in fishing, and 111 boats, 261 men, and 26 boys only partially so engaged.

Fish generally captured—Turbot, sole, plaice, conger, mackerel, hake, cod, pollock, whiting, bream, gurnard, sprats, and oysters.

The fishing is by means of trawls, long lines, hand lines, and seines.

Mackerel appeared in quantities in August and September, close to the shore, off Ringabella. Not adequate means of capture.

Lobsters and crabs were taken, but not in any great quantity.

The fishermen are reported orderly. Nothing of any importance has occurred since report for 1877.

Kinsale Division.

From Myrtleville Point, East, to Galley Head, West; a distance of 110 miles.

Unguarded portions :—From Barry's Head to Flat Head (Oyster Haven) 1¾ miles; from Muckroes to Virgin Mary Point, Dunny Cove, 3 miles 130 yards; total 4 miles, 1,500 yards.

In 1878 there were 342 boats, 1,632 men, and 107 boys reported to have been engaged in the sea fisheries, viz. :—60 first-class boats, 111 second-class, and 171 third-class. Of these 84 boats, 487 men, and 47 boys were solely engaged in fishing, and 258 boats, 1,145 men, and 60 boys as only partially engaged.

The fish found in the greatest quantities off this division are mackerel, herring, sprats, pilchards, bream, pollock, cod, hake, soles, whitings, and scad, and a few oysters.

Large shoals of pilchards, mackerel, scad, and herrings were seen off the coast from June to September, but the principal mackerel fishery is from March to June.

Lobsters and crabs were taken in fair quantities, and the supply is said to be increasing.

In last report mention was made that application had been made with the view of having the Storm Drum Signals established at Kinsale—this has been accomplished, and is in working order at Summer Cove, Kinsale.

Fishermen throughout the division are reported to have been well behaved.

Skibbereen Division.

From Galley Head to Snave Bridge—about 170 miles.

Unguarded about 70 miles, viz., Three Castles Head to Carberry Island, Carberry Island to Snave Bridge; from Rinks Castle to Ballydehob, besides the Islands of Clear, Sherkin, Ringarogy, Long, Castle, Horse, and other smaller ones, occasionally visited.

The returns from Coastguard show that in 1878 there were 272 boats, 1,226 men, and 29 boys employed in the sea fisheries; of these 77 boats, 322 men, and 10 boys, have been solely engaged in fishing; and 195 boats, 904 men, and 19 boys, partially engaged.

Fish generally taken are cod, ling, mackerel, hake, pollock, bream, pilchards, and scad.

Modes of fishing—seines, hand and long lines, trawls, drift nets, and trammels.

Pilchards, in July, August, and September, appeared off the coast in large shoals, and a considerable number were captured.

Shoals, also, of mackerel and herrings were seen at various times from May to July.

Considerable quantities of lobsters have been taken in this division, and the capture of lobsters and crabs is reported to have been very large.

The fishermen reported to have been well behaved throughout this division.

Castletown Division.

From Kenmare Bridge to Snave Bridge, Bantry Bay.

A considerable portion of the coast in this Division is unguarded, viz. :—From Carriglass to Snave Bridge, 16 miles; Clanderry Head to Kenmare, 14 miles; Cod's Head to Ardelaggan Point, 4 miles; Garrinish Bay to Dursey, 6 miles; Dursey Head to Pulleen 7 miles.

The returns show that in 1878 there were 133 boats, 689 men, and 10 boys, engaged in the sea fisheries, viz., solely engaged in fishing, 6 boats and 23 men; only partially engaged, 127 boats, 666 men, and 10 boys.

The fish in general frequenting the coast are mackerel, pilchards, herrings, cod, ling, hake, pollock, whiting, &c.

Modes of capture—seines, herring nets, long lines, and hand lines.

The fishing during the year has not been as good as during the year 1877, but off the Dursey Island it is reported that large quantities of mackerel were taken late in the season.

Herrings and pilchards were seen in large shoals off the Allihies ground, but the fishermen were not provided with proper means for their capture.

A few lobsters were taken.

The fishermen are reported to have been quiet and orderly.

Killarney Division.

From Kenmare Bridge, south, to Blennerville Bridge, near Tralee, north.

Length of coast line, 281 miles. Unguarded 56 miles, viz. :—Inch to Castlemaine, 14 miles; Slea Head to Cloger Head and the Blaskets, 8 miles; Brandon Creek to Blennerville and Maharees, 34 miles. Total, 56 miles.

By the Coastguard returns there were 314 boats, 1,395 men and 9 boys, engaged in the sea fisheries, viz. :—Solely engaged in fishing 133 boats and 478 men; partially engaged, 181 boats, 917 men, and 9 boys.

The kinds of fish generally captured is—turbot, soles, bream, brit, plaice, cod, ling, hake, pollock, shad, mackerel, pilchards, &c.

Fish it is reported were generally scarce throughout the district during 1878.

Large shoals of mackerel and pilchards were seen off Ballydavid Guard. Quantities of herrings, mackerel, and pilchards were seen, and the captures were considerable.

A considerable quantity of lobsters were taken during the year.

The fishermen are reported as orderly and well behaved.

Ballyheigue Division.

From Blennerville, County Kerry, to Foynes, County Limerick.

Extent of division, seventy-five miles, of which there are forty-nine unguarded.

There are 88 boats registered, viz., 1 first-class, 34 second, and 53 third-class; and crews of 257 men and 3 boys. Of these boats there are solely engaged in fishing 9 second and 9 third-class, and only partially engaged, 1 first, 25 second, and 53 third-class. This return shows an increase of 5 boats during the year. Very little fishing is carried on in this division; the chief place where fish are caught is in Tralee Bay. The people are generally small farmers, and only follow fishing occasionally. The modes of fishing are long lines and drift nets for herrings. A large shoal of the latter and mackerel appeared on the Kerry shore of the Shannon in September, and a good many were captured; but owing to the weather becoming very bad the fishing could not be continued and the fish disappeared. No mackerel were taken, as there are no mackerel nets in this locality. Large shoals appeared from five to seven miles off Tralee Bay in August, and many were captured.

A few lobsters were caught off Kerry Head. The fishermen are generally orderly and peaceable.

Oyster Fisheries.

There are large public banks in Tralee Bay and in the Shannon at Tarbert, Ballydonohoe, Ballylongford, Kiltiery, Lougrock, and Carrigeens. They are not improving, and so far as can be ascertained, very little spatting during the past season. Bye-laws are in force, prohibiting the taking of small oysters, but from other onerous duties the Coast Guard find it very difficult to enforce them, and there is no other authority to do so. They frequently overhaul the boats dredging. Some of the private oyster beds in this division are doing well, and the oysters bring a very high price in the market. A large quantity has been imported from France, and the experiment is reported to be successful. The oysters from one private bank bring as much as 15s. a hundred, delivered at the railway station in Tralee, so good is the quality considered.

SEAFIELD DIVISION, COUNTY CLARE.

From Ballycrinon to Cancapple Head.

Extent of division, about 149 miles, of which about 67 are unguarded.

There are registered in this division 155 boats, with crews amounting to 411 men and 4 boys. Of these there are only 14 boats (third-class) and 42 men solely engaged in fishing; and partially engaged, 1 second and 140 third-class boats, with crews amounting to 369 men and 4 boys. This shows an increase of boats registered in the division of 11 boats and 41 men.

Cappa Station.—Ballymacrinon to Querrin. The only fish captured are herrings, and only in small quantities, which are captured by drift nets; no trawling carried on. A small quantity of oysters is taken from Moyne to Querrin, a distance of about six miles, during the season, under £100 worth. The beds are not improving. Unguarded portion of coast at this station about three miles.

Kilcredane Station.—Querrin to Bealnaglass. The fish generally captured are herrings, mackerel, and ling, lobsters and crabs. Large shoals of herrings appeared in July, August, and September, but few were captured. Large shoals of mackerel also appeared to the N.E. of Loop Head in October, but owing to bad weather the canoes could not venture out more than two or three nights, although the people had their mackerel nets ready. The fishermen in this locality suffer particularly from want of a little improvement being made at a place called Goleen, which could be made, at a small expense, a safe place of shelter for the canoes, many of which frequent the harbour. If this were carred out it would be a great incentive to the fishermen, and a large quantity of mackerel, which is now lost, might be taken in the season. Unguarded portion about thirty-seven miles.

Kilkee Station.—Bealnaglass to Doonbeg, about 16 miles.

Cod, ling, and mackerel are the principal fish captured. Large shoals of mackerel appeared close to the shore from August to October. With few exceptions the fishermen are well supplied with means for their capture. Large quantities of very fine lobsters and crabs were captured this year at Kilkee and Farrihy; it is impossible to ascertain, even approximately, the quantity. Unguarded—about thirteen miles.

Seafield Station.—From Doonbeg to Spanish Point.

Bream, ling, mackerel, and lobsters are the descriptions of fish generally captured. Large shoals of mackerel appeared in September and October, about two and a half miles from shore. The people have adequate means for their capture; the weather, however, was against them. Large quantities of lobsters and crabs were captured north and south of Mutton Island. Unguarded—about three miles.

Liscannor Station.—From Spanish Point to Cancapple.

Bream, cod, and ling, are the principal descriptions of fish captured; canoes only employed. Lobsters and crabs were taken in a small quantity this year. They abound on the coast, but the difficulty of getting them to market is the great drawback to any improvement. No steps have been as yet taken to remove the rock which is so dangerous at the mouth of the Liscannor Harbour. Unguarded—about twelve miles.

The fishermen in the whole division are reported to be peaceable and orderly.

Oyster Fisheries.

The principal public banks are in Clonderlaw Bay, and they are not improving. Great difficulty exists in enforcing the bye-laws preventing the capture of small oysters, the Coast Guard stations being so far away from the beds, and there being no other authority to do so.

Galway Division.

Canamallagh Point, county Clare, to Mace Head, county Galway.

There are registered in this division 444 vessels and boats, with crews of 1,103 men and 34 boys. They embrace of first-class, 10 vessels and 40 men and 10 boys; of second-class, 6 boats and 24 men; and of third-class, 54 boats and 130 men, all being solely engaged in fishing; while there are only partially so engaged of second-class, 182 boats, with 571 men and 10 boys; and of third-class, 191 boats and 338 men and 14 boys. Both the quantity and quality of fish in Galway Bay has improved, as is evidenced by the addition of three trawlers to the fleet, and the well-stocked state of the fish market during the season.

Ballyvaughan Station, guarded.—Black Head to Muckinish Castle, about 10 miles, unguarded from Canamallagh Point to Black Head, and from Muckinish to Claren Bridge, a distance of about 60 miles. The principal descriptions of fish captured are cod, ling, bream, whiting, mackerel, and herrings. The trawling vessels belonging to Galway work also along this shore and round Black Head, and get the finest descriptions of flat-fish. In November and December they get large quantities of very fine plaice inside Glenina. Large shoals of mackerel in July, August, and September, off this coast, but no means of capture except hand lines, and few consequently taken. A slight show of pilchards also, but hardly any herrings made their appearance this year. The capture of round fish by the long lines was better than for many years past. There are 7 boats fishing for lobsters at Glenina and Murrough, and it is estimated that each boat gets about 2 dozen weekly, for which they get from 7*s.* to 10*s.* a dozen during the season. This does not prevent them carrying on other fishing at the same time. In the neighbourhood of Glenina or Murrough accommodation for canoes is greatly required, and improvements might be made at a very inconsiderable cost. At Finvarra a depot for lobsters, crabs and other shell-fish is about being established by an enterprising English firm, who will purchase any shell-fish offered to them in good condition. Crabs abound on this coast, but are not taken, as no sale for them. The opening of this depot will develop a trade in them. There have been no conflicts between the fishermen, who are orderly and peaceable. The trawlers, however, sometimes do great injury to the long lines, dragging through them. It is difficult to avoid them when they are not properly buoyed.

There are several public oyster banks on this coast. They are situated in Tyrone, Kinvarra, and Oranmore Bays; they are not improved. In Tyrone Bay about 45 boats dredged, and in the early part of the season realized from £1 to £1 15*s.* each per day, but in the latter portion only from 7*s.* 6*d.* to 10*s.* each boat. Very little were taken off Crusheen or Oranmore beds. There was only one month allowed for dredging on the public beds last year, and the weather was too severe to allow dredging to be much carried on during that month—December. There are also a number of private oyster banks in this district, but they are all fattening beds, and produce no spat. About £7,000 worth of oysters annually sold off them. In some places the French oysters have done remarkably well. Complaints are still made of the depredations committed by persons going along the shores in the neighbourhood of private beds, under pretence of gathering winkles, cockles, mussels, &c., and the expense of protecting the oysters is so great that it debars proprietors from laying out capital in more extensive cultivation. It is said these pickers carry away large quantities of oysters, even from beds held under a license. This is certainly a great drawback to a proper system of oyster cultivation.

Barna Station.—Claren Bridge to Crumlin, a distance of about 30 miles; unguarded from Claren Bridge to Blackrock, about 14 miles.

The principal fish captured are turbot, brit, sole, hake, glassen, and mackerel. Very good trawling ground, which is availed of by a large and successful fleet of trawlers. Large shoals of herrings and mackerel appeared in February and September. The herrings used to be caught with a rod and line off the pier at Barna; they were generally of a small description, and the nets were not suitable for them. Small quantities of lobsters and crabs were taken. The fishermen are peaceable and orderly.

The oyster fisheries are said to be improving. There were about 60 boats engaged at dredging, and earned from £4 to £5 each boat.

Costello Station.—Crumlin to Mace Head, about 120 miles; unguarded from Rossaneel to Mace Head, about 104 miles.

The principal fish are cod, ling, hake, pollock, pilchards, and mackerel. Mackerel are sometimes in great abundance. They appeared in large shoals in August and September close inshore, but the means of capture were not at all suitable. There is good trawling ground along the coast, which is fully worked. Lobsters and crabs are caught in large quantities. The crabs are not sold; they would not pay the carriage to market.

There are several private oyster beds in this division, but it is difficult to ascertain with any degree of accuracy in what state they are or the quantity of oysters sold. It is estimated at about £20,000 worth.

Arran Island Station.—In these islands there was an increase of 6 boats registered during the year, the total being 3 second and 40 third-class. Of these there were only 2 second and 29 third-class boats solely engaged in fishing, the rest only partially so. Large shoals of mackerel appeared during August, but the means of capture were totally inadequate. Cod, ling, and bream are the principal fish captured. A small quantity of lobsters are taken round North Arran, and at South Arran.

In the whole of the district the fishermen are spoken of as peaceable and orderly, and no conflicts.

Since the trawling boundary has been removed the trawlers have taken large quantities of plaice inside the line, within which trawling was prohibited for many years, but they really only frequent that part of the bay during the short period when plaice set in.

They find it more profitable to trawl outside.

Clifden Division.

Mason Island, County Galway, to Doaghbeg, County Mayo.

In this division there were registered 657 boats, employing 1,865 men and 48 boys, which were composed of 220 second and 437 third-class, all only partially engaged in fishing. This shows an increase of 116 boats in the division. The division extends for about 261 miles, out of which there are about 191 miles unguarded—the islands of Boffin, Shark, Turk, and nearly all the islands in Clew Bay.

Roundstone Station.—Mason Island to Ballinlina, about 62 miles; unguarded from Mason Island to Fishery Bridge, Ballyconneely, about 41 miles.

The principal fish taken are cod, ling, bream, and congers. Large shoals of mackerel and herrings appear off the coast every harvest, but there are no nets kept ready for their capture. A quantity of fine lobsters are taken, but not many crabs. It is stated that about 3,900 dozen of lobsters were taken during the season.

There are no public oyster banks on this part of the coast.

Bayleek Station.—Slyne Head to Streamstown, a distance of about 30 miles; unguarded from Clifdon to Slyne Head, about 17 miles; also the islands.

The same modes of fishing and descriptions of fish as on other parts of this coast. Fishing not carried on regularly as a business. No shoals of fish have been seen off this part of the coast during the year. Very small quantities of lobsters are taken, but fishermen go to the county Mayo coast for this fishing, and remain out several weeks at a time in their open boats.

Cleggan Station.—From Streamstown to Renvyle, about 25 miles; unguarded from Streamstown to Weir, and from Letterfrack to Renvylo, about 13 miles.

Bream, skad, and mackerel are the principal fish captured. A few small shoals of mackerel appeared inshore in August and September; few captured. Only a small quantity of lobsters are taken.

There are private oyster beds in this division, some of which are reported as doing well.

Tully Station.—Renvyle to Roonagh, about 30 miles; unguarded from Rowa to Roonagh, about 20 miles. Mackerel, herrings, bream, coalfish, cod, and pollock are the principal descriptions of fish captured. Large shoals of mackerel appeared during August and September about a mile from the shore, and in Killary Bay, but the nets are not sufficient for their capture. About 100 dozen of lobsters were taken in the season.

Pigeon Point Station.—From Roonagh to Doaghbeg, a distance of about 114 miles; unguarded about 100 miles from Roonagh Head to Westport, and from Rosmoney to Doaghbeg, and all islands. Herrings, mackerel, bream, cod, ling, and pollock are the principal descriptions of fish taken. No large shoals have appeared this year off this part of the coast.

In the whole district the fishermen are reported as peaceable and orderly. No conflicts.

Keel Division.

From Doaghbeg to Doona, County Mayo, about 170 miles.

In this division there are registered 57 third-class boats, employing 122 men and 4 boys, all only partially engaged in fishing.

The past season off this part of the coast has been a bad one, the quantity of fish taken being much less than that of previous years. The fishermen are, as a rule, employed about farming, and only occasionally fish when it suits their purpose. The greater part of the men go to other parts of the kingdom early in spring, and do not return till autumn. The fishing is therefore greatly neglected, and the result is that only a small quantity of fish is captured, though it is thought by many the fish are as numerous as ever. Some, however, think they are not as plentiful.

Achilbeg Station.—Achilbeg to Doaghbeg and to Dooega, about 28 miles. Cod, whiting, and bream are the principal fish; cod principally in December, January, and February; whiting in April, May, and June. There was a very fair season in lobsters by the county Galway men, who frequent this part of the coast.

Keele Station.—From Dooega to Ridge Point, about 33 miles. Bream, pollock, congers, and mackerel are the fish most abundant. In July, August, and September large shoals of mackerel and herrings appeared about a mile from the shore; but there are not adequate means for their capture, as the fishermen have not craft or gear suitable. Only a small quantity of lobsters captured during the season.

Bullsmouth Station.—From Ridge Point to Achil Sound on the west, and from Doona Head to Ballacraher Bay on the east. None of the boats at this station fished for the purpose of sale during the year. Pollock is the principal fish taken.

In the whole division the fishermen are peaceable and orderly. No conflicts.

Belmullet Division.

From Doona Head to Butter Point, about 73 miles.

The same observations as in previous division are applicable to this. Fishing is only carried on occasionally, when it suits the people, who are mostly farmers. There are registered 183 third-class boats, employing 505 men; but they are all only partially engaged in fishing.

Claggan Station.—Geesalia to Belmullet, about 20 miles; unguarded, Geesalia to Doolough, about 2 miles. Small shoals of herring and mackerel appeared in August and September, half a mile to one mile off the shore. Nets not sufficient for their capture.

Tullaghan Station.—Geesalia to Monley's Point and round Doohoma, about 14 miles; unguarded from Goolamone to Doona Head, about 10 miles. Herrings are the principal fish taken, but no shoals appeared off the coast. Very little fishing done.

Ballyglass Station.—Erris Head to Shanahee Point, about 12 miles; unguarded, Seal Island to Butter Point, about 10 miles. Cod, ling, turbot, gurnard, pollock, mackerel and herrings, are the principal fish taken. In April large quantities of mackerel were captured, and since then smaller quantities of mackerel and herring, from about 200 yards to 1 mile from the shore in Broadhaven Bay. The means of capture are not adequate. Large quantities of lobsters taken by the county Galway men, who come round in the season.

Elly Bay Station.—From Ardelly Point to Annagh Head, about 15 miles; unguarded about 8 miles from back shore of Elly Bay to Annagh Head. Herrings, mackerel, and whiting are the principal descriptions of fish taken. Large shoals of herrings and mackerel appeared in July and October. The means of capture are not sufficient. Lobsters taken in large quantity by the county Galway men.

In the whole division the fishermen are reported as peaceable and orderly.

Ballycastle, County Mayo, Division.

From Butter Point, Broadhaven, to Bartragh Gap, Killala.

In this division there are registered 104 boats, employing 501 men, all third-class, and only partially engaged in fishing. Like the neighbouring districts, the people, for the most part, only fish as occasion suits. Although there is fine trawling ground, no trawler is employed for the purpose of capturing for sale. The only vessel that trawls is a yacht belonging to Sir Charles Gore, bart., who fishes for amusement, and takes a quantity of fine fish.

Ross Station.—Gap of Bartragh to Palmerstown Bridge, about 6 miles. Pollock, plaice, sole, mackerel, and herrings are the principal descriptions of fish taken. Mackerel appeared in large quantities in July and August, but the means of taking them were not sufficient. Herrings appeared in September in large shoals, and were captured in large quantities from a quarter to a mile off the shore.

Kilcummin Station.—Rathfran to Ballycastle, about 10 miles; unguarded, Lacken to Downpatrick Head, about 4 miles. Herrings and mackerel are the principal fish captured. Large shoals appeared from July to September, from 1 to 2 miles off shore; but there were no adequate means of capture. Lobsters and crabs were plentiful during the season, but no sale for crabs.

Ballycastle Station.—There are 7 boats at this station, registered by the Collector of Customs, that did not fish during the past year. Very little fishing carried on in this guard; pollock and coarse ground fish are those principally taken. A few lobsters were also captured by three boats from the county Galway.

Belderrig Station.—From Brandy Point to Glenulra, about 30 miles; unguarded about 16 miles. Mackerel is the principal fish taken, and large shoals appeared in August and September about two miles off the shore, but there were no adequate means for their capture. Fishing only very partially carried on on this coast.

Portacloy Station.—The same remarks as the former station apply equally to this, save that at Portacloy a large quantity of lobsters were taken.

Pullendiva.

From Bartragh to Coney's Island, Sligo. About 59 miles.

In this division there are registered 46 boats, employing 165 men and 7 boys, all third-class boats, 10 of them only being solely engaged in fishing, and 36 only partially so. The men who fish along this coast have but bad boats and worse gear, and in consequence of no pier or shelter they seldom venture more than a few hundred yards from the shore. There has been a fair take of lobsters during the season—nearly 18,000, as nearly as could be ascertained, having been sent to market. There was also a fair take of pollock, and a few herrings, mackerel, and whiting. A boat slip is much required at Enniscrone, and some improvement also effected at Dromore Bay, as the boats are often damaged waiting for assistance up the beach, which is very steep. Since the introduction of loans an impetus has been given to fishing in parts of this coast, particularly for lobsters.

Enniscrone Station.—Ballina to Carrenduff, about 12 miles. Herrings, mackerel, whiting, sole, brit, turbot are the principal descriptions of fish taken. Herrings in the largest quantities; more turbot has been taken last season than for many years past. A good quantity of lobsters were also taken at Lacken and Carrowhubbuck.

Pullochecney Station.—Carnduff to Easkey, about 7 miles. Mackerel and herrings are the principal fish, and they appeared in large shoals in July and August close inshore, and were captured in large quantities. There are better means for capture here, but the nets require to be made deeper. A good quantity of lobsters were taken

Pullendiva Station.—Easkey to Dunmoran, about 13 miles. Herrings, mackerel, and pollock are the principal descriptions of fish taken, but herrings in the largest quantities. Several large shoals of mackerel appeared in June and July off Dromore, and herrings in September, but very few were taken in consequence of insufficient gear. A very fair catch of lobsters took place. They were sent principally to the Dublin markets. It is reported that there is plenty of fish along this coast, but the people have not the means to procure boats and gear.

Derkmore Station.—Dunmoran to Coney's Island, about 25 miles. Pollock, flat-fish, cod, gurnard, and herrings are the principal descriptions taken, but all only in small quantities. A few shoals of herrings appeared off Dunmoran in August and September close inshore, but only a small quantity were captured.

A good quantity of lobsters of a very good quality were taken during the season, as near as can be ascertained, about 300 dozen, which were sold from 7*s.* 6*d.* to 8*s.* 6*d.* per dozen.

There is a public oyster bank in this guard which is said to be improving, and that the spatting was greater last than the previous season; however, only a small quantity, about £50 worth, is taken.

There are some important private oyster beds in the division.

In the whole division the fishermen are reported as peaceable and orderly.

Sligo District

Strandhill, Sligo, to Donegal Abbey.

In this division there were 139 boats registered, employing 577 men and 8 boys, of which there were 1 first, 13 second, and 17 third-class solely engaged in fishing, and 9 second and 99 third-class only partially so engaged. This shows a reduction of 10 boats since last return, which has been caused by 8 boats at Rosse's Point and 2 at Rockley being broken up or their registers returned, as the boats are not used for the purposes of fishing for sale. The return now made approaches accuracy more than those of former years. The fisheries in this division are reported as decreasing. The long line fishing at Mullaghmore was not so good during the past year, and there has been hardly any herring or mackerel fishing. The fishermen at Bunnatrohan, Co. Donegal, are at a great loss for some refuge for their boats.

Rosse's Point Station.—Strandhill to Drumcliffe, 18 miles; unguarded, Strandhill to Sligo, and Lower Rosse's Point to Drumcliffe, about 11 miles.

Oyster dredging is really the only regular description of fishing practised. A public bed exists in Sligo river, but it is not improving. It has been stated that it is hardly worth while dredging now, so few oysters are taken in the season. Cod, ling, pollock, &c., are taken in large quantities by the Rockley fishermen. Some large shoals of herrings appeared off the coast during September, and they are looked for from that time till February.

Rockley Station.—Drumcliffe to Cullimore Point, about 17 miles; unguarded, Drumcliffe to Lissadill, about 6 miles.

Flat-fish, cod, ling, mackerel, and herrings are the principal fish captured. Large shoals of mackerel appeared off the coast during August and September, about half a mile off the shore.

There were no adequate means of capture. Herrings appeared in October and were captured in some quantity, but nothing of any consequence. A good quantity of very fine lobsters and crabs were captured off Ballyconnell, Brown's Bay, and Rockley. At the latter place the harbour which was originally built at the public expense, and was transferred to the Grand Jury, is being allowed to get into a state of delapidation, and it is stated will be a great loss to the fishermen.

Mullaghmore Station.—Streedagh to Bundoran, including Innishmurray Island, about 23 miles, and 8 to the Island; unguarded, Streedagh to Rockuragh and Bunduff to Bundoran, about 18 miles.

The same descriptions of fish are taken on this part of the coast. Several small shoals of mackerel, but no herrings or pilchards, appeared in Mullaghmore Bay about half a mile off, in August, but the nets used are not deep enough unless the fish come close inshore.

Large quantities of lobsters were taken, but they were found in largest quantities by the Mullaghmore men off the coast along Derkmore, Pullendiva, Pullocheeney and Enniscrone, and Innismurray Island. There are four private oyster beds in this guard, but they are not improving.

Ballyshannon Station.—Bundoran to Eske River, Donegal, about 30 miles; unguarded nearly the whole coast.

Herrings, mackerel, cod, ling, plaice, whiting, and bream are the fish taken. Small shoals only of herrings and mackerel appeared this year a quarter to two miles off the shore. No quantity was captured. Lobsters and crabs were captured in good quantity at Kildoney and Bunnatroohan. At the latter place the harbour requires something of improvement to afford shelter for boats. At present it is in a bad state of repair and a great loss to the fishermen, being their only place of refuge on this part of the coast. The fishermen complain also that they are not allowed to reap any of the advantages offered to fishermen in the neighbouring county by loans for repairs of boats and providing suitable fishing gear.

In the whole division the fishermen are peaceable and orderly, and no conflicts.

Killybegs Division.

From Donegal Quay to Lower Ferry, East, county Donegal.

There were, in this division, in 1878, 168 boats, employing 783 men, and 53 boys, as compared with 145 boats, 680 men, and 88 boys, in 1877.

Nets and long and hand lines are the means of capture.

Herrings, mackerel, whiting, cod, and other fish are taken.

The boats, however, in this district are too small for successful fishing, and the gear requires to be better in order to enable the fishermen to pursue their avocation at a greater distance from the coast.

Lobster fishing has been good throughout the district, and very considerable quantities of lobsters have been caught during the season.

The fishermen are very orderly.

The extent of coast line is 140 miles, of which about 16 miles are unguarded.

Guidore Division.

From Gweebarra Bar to Mullaghdoo.

There were, in this division, in 1878, 42 boats, employing 133 men, and 10 boys, as compared with 37 boats, 104 men, and 13 boys, in 1877.

Nets and long and hand lines are the means of capture.

Large quantities of mackerel were seen round the islands in June, July, and August, but, from want of adequate means of capture, including a larger class of boats, very few were taken.

Lobsters and crabs were captured in large quantities—more than £1,000 worth having been sold during the season.

The conduct of the fishermen was excellent.

The extent of coast line is 33 miles, of which about 12 miles are unguarded.

Rathmullin Division.

From Lough Swilly to Bloody Foreland.

There were in this Division, in 1878, 186 boats, employing 345 men and 23 boys, as compared with 158 boats, 423 men, and 31 boys in 1877.

Herring and mackerel have appeared in large quantities off some portions of the coast, but were not captured in any numbers, in consequence of adequate means not existing. Cod, ling, flounders, and other fish, are taken.

Lobsters and crabs were not taken in any considerable quantity, so far as can be ascertained, except round the coast of Horn Head and Sheephaun Bay. The fishermen have been orderly in their conduct.

In this district, also, the fishing might be largely developed if suitable boats and gear were provided.

The extent of coast line is 120 miles, of which about 25 are unguarded.

Moville Division.

From Inch Embankment, county Donegal, to Magilligan Point, county Derry.

There were in this District, in 1878, 213 boats, with 768 men and 4 boys, as compared with 118 boats, 626 men, and 4 boys in 1877, as recorded in last Report.

Hand and long lines are used in the capture of fish.

Turbot, bream, cod, whiting, and other fish were taken in considerable quantities, and herring in a less degree.

Lobsters and crabs were captured in considerable quantities in the localities of Portnasantally and Portaleen. About 2,016 lobsters and 15,524 crabs were taken in these places; and about 1,920 lobsters and 2,400 crabs were taken by four boats, between Stroove Head and Tremone Head.

It is to be regretted that a disposition has been shown by some of the fishermen in Lough Foyle to encroach on the several fisheries in pursuit of salmon. This has given the Coast Guards some trouble, as they have not sufficient men at the stations to ensure proper inspection of fishing boats at night.

The extent of coast line is 36 miles, of which 22 are unguardod.

Oyster Fisheries.

The oyster banks, between Roe River and Clare River, are not improving.

Ballycastle Division.

From Downhill, County Londonderry, to Jenny's Bridge, County Antrim.

There were 140 boats, 270 men, and 4 boys employed in 1878, as compared with 143 boats, 263 men, and 6 boys, in 1877.

Draft-nets, long lines and hand lines are employed in the capture of fish.

Mackerel, pollock, cod, ling, bream, and skate are taken in some quantity.

Lobsters and crabs are caught in considerable numbers, principally between Gob Colliery and Fair Head.

The fishermen of this district are orderly and peaceful.

The immense destruction of river fish, by pollution of flax water throughout the country, has been supplemented here by the loss, in one instance, from this cause, of 100 crabs, near the mouth of the Margy river. Lieutenant Chapman, R.N., in an interesting letter, deals ably with this subject.

The extent of coast line is about 55 miles, of which about nine are unguarded.

CARRICKFERGUS DIVISION.

From Jenny's Bridge to Fort William Park, near Belfast.

In this district, 51 boats, 114 men, and 4 boys were engaged in fishing, in 1878, as compared with 47 boats and 95 men in 1877.

The modes of capture are seines, long lines, hand lines, rods, draft nets, herring nets, and trawls. There is good trawling ground all over Belfast Lough, and it is greatly taken advantage of.

Shoals of herrings appeared off the coast at Ballygally about the middle of August, and very large shoals of herrings appeared off the coast at Whitehead in June and July; but there were no adequate means of capture. Cod, ling, sole, and pollock are also taken.

Lobster and crabs were captured in large quantities in Carnlough and Glenarm Bays: about 4,000 of each were taken during the year.

The fishermen are very orderly and well-conducted.

The extent of coast line is 53 miles, no portion of which is unguarded.

Oyster Fisheries.

Oysters are taken all over Belfast Lough. There is one public bed, about one mile in extent, S.S.E from Whitehead. The amount realized from the oysters taken during the year was about £900. The oysters are generally large, but small quantities of a lesser size are also sold.

DONAGHADEE DIVISION.

From Tillysburn Head, County Antrim, to Newcastle Quay, County Down.

During 1878, 124 boats, 392 men, and 28 boys were employed, as against 105 boats, 360 men, and 10 boys in 1877.

The modes of fishing practiced are by hand lines, long lines, occasional trawling, drift nets, and seine nets.

Cod, plaice, whiting, pollock, and, in some places, herring are captured. Shoals of herring appeared during the summer about three miles from shore, off Millisle, but were not taken in any quantity from want of adequate means of capture.

About £100 worth of lobsters and crabs were taken during the season by four Groomsport boats; and a small number in the Millisle locality.

The fishermen in this district are orderly. The extent of coast line is 44 miles.

STRANGFORD DIVISION.

From Newcastle Quay to Sheepland Head.

In 1878, 107 boats, 189 men, and 10 boys were employed, as against 101 boats, 165 men, and 15 boys in 1877.

The modes of capture are nets and hand lines. There is no trawling.

Herrings, mackerel, and cod were taken.

Lobsters and crabs were not taken in large quantities. For three months in the year, about one hundred a week were taken, off Killard Point.

The conduct of the fishermen was good.

Oyster Fisheries.

No oysters were sold in the district this season. Strangford Lough used to produce a considerable quantity of oysters; and it is hoped that their culture may be taken up again, and banks stocked and preserved. Many facilities are afforded, by Strangford Lough, for the successful production of oysters.

NEWCASTLE DIVISION.

From Sheepland Head to Riverfoot, Kilkeel.

There were employed, in this district, in 1878, 157 boats, 642 men and 33 boys, as compared with 141 boats, 521 men, and 29 boys, in 1877.

The modes of capture are by trammel nets, hand lines, and long lines.

The herring fishery, in connection with Ardglass, is referred to elsewhere. There is good trawling ground six miles S.E. of Annalong, which has lately been much used.

Turbot, whiting, mackerel, haddock, cod, ling, sole, plaice, and other fish are caught largely off Ardglass.

This harbour is now being carried towards completion, and will be of incalculable advantage, not only to the district, but to the country at large.

Lobsters and crabs were taken, in some quantities, in the neighbourhood of Ringfad Point. About 500 of the former, and 1,000 of the latter were captured. About the same number was taken between Annalong and Black Rock.

The fishermen in the district are orderly.

The extent of the coast is about 42 miles, no part of which is unguarded.

Carlingford Division.

From Riverfoot, Kilkeel, county Down, to Maiden Tower, Drogheda.

In 1878, 266 boats, 876 men, and 68 boys were employed, as compared with 277 boats, 915 men, and 52 boys, in 1877.

The modes of capture are nets and long lines.

Mussels are taken in considerable quantities in the River Boyne.

Herrings, cod, plaice, turbot, and whiting are captured.

Lobsters and crabs, in certain portions of the district, are reported to be taken in some numbers, though accurate returns have not been obtained.

The conduct of the fishermen generally has been orderly. An exception seems to have occurred in the Carlingford Coast-guard Station, where fishermen from Arklow made themselves troublesome.

The extent of the coast is about 85 miles, of which about 2 miles are unguarded.

Oyster Fisheries.

The principal public oyster fisheries are in Rostrevor Bay, and from the Black Rock to Ballyonan Quay. They are said to be improving, and the spatting was greater than in 1877.

Malahide Division.

From Laytown to Baldoyle.

In 1878, 96 boats, 452 men, and 22 boys were employed, as compared with 93 boats, 426 men, and 18 boys, in 1877.

The modes of capture are trawling, long lines, hand lines, and herring nets.

Herrings, turbot, plaice, cod, and ling are taken.

Lobsters and crabs have been taken in the Skerries district.

Trawling within the limits has prevailed to a considerable extent, and it is desirable that increased efforts should be made to put down this practice. The Coast Guard will, no doubt, continue their exertions in this direction.

The extent of the coast is about 26 miles, none of which is unguarded.

Irish Reproductive Loan Fund.

Mr. Brady's Report for the Counties of Leitrim, Sligo, Mayo, Galway, Clare, Limerick, and part of Kerry.

County Leitrim.

In this county there was a sum of £332 available for loans for the year 1878. There was one application received for £10, and it was recommended, but was never taken up by the borrower, and was therefore cancelled. Only a few persons living on the small seaboard of this county follow fishing.

County Sligo.

In this county there was a sum of £449 available for the year.

There were 82 applications received from 41 persons, amounting to £551 12*s.* 6*d.* There were only 19 loans recommended, amounting to £275, and out of this sum only £267 were issued, the balance not having been taken up. In one case out of these I was obliged to recommend the loan of £24 to be recalled in consequence of the money not having been properly applied. The loans ranged from £5 to £24, and were on the whole fairly expended. I had some difficulty in causing a proper expenditure in some cases, and I have felt obliged to recommend that no further loans should be given to certain persons who had already obtained loans in consequence of the manner in which their former loans were expended.

When the money has been fairly expended on the matters for which it was lent, it has proved of incalculable benefit to the fishermen.

There have been no arrears of payment of instalments of the loans made in either 1877 or 1878, but there are three cases of loans made in 1875 where the instalments are in arrear, amounting to £12 0*s.* 6*d.*, and three of those made in 1876, amounting to £5 11*s.* 7*d.*, making a total of arrears of £17 12*s.* 1*d.* up to 31st December last.

The total amount issued in this county for four years was £1,078, out of which there have been repaid £565 10*s.* 11*d.*

County Mayo.

The amount available for this county was £600.

There were 88 applications received from 168 persons, amounting to £1,373. Out of these there were 51 loans recommended, amounting to £622. There were 2 loans afterwards cancelled amounting to £28. The total amount issued on account of these loans was £558. The balance of £36 was not taken up by the applicants, and was therefore cancelled. The loans ranged from £5 to £36.

On the whole, so far as I have been able to ascertain up to the present, the money issued was fairly expended, and proved of great use to the people.

The persons to whom loans were made in this county are of a miserably poor class, and it is not at all surprising that there should be arrears of repayments in many cases. Still, considering their poverty and the depressed state of the country during the year, I do not think that the arrears are excessive. There were out of loans made in 1875, instalments in arrears on the 31st December last, in 6 cases, amounting to £23 16*s.* 8*d.*; out of loans made in 1876, instalments in arrears in 6 cases amounting to £22 4*s.* 5*d.*; out of loans made in 1877, instalments in arrears in 2 cases, amounting to £4 2*s.* 4*d.*; no arrears of loans made in 1878. Total of arrears in the county, £50 3*s.* 5*d.* Although this amount is small, I cannot understand why it should be left overdue. In one case an instalment is due since August, 1876. Very close inquiry was made as to the solvency of the sureties before making the loans, and I believe in very few cases will it be found that they are insufficient, if proper steps be taken to enforce payment.

The total amount issued for the 4 years in this county was £2,636, out of which there have been repaid £1,383 2*s.* 2*d.* One loan made in 1877, amounting to £12, was recalled in consequence of the money not having been properly applied.

Co. Galway.

There was a sum of £1,077 available for this county for the year 1878. There were 188 applications received from 401 persons, amounting to £3,667 19*s.*, out of which there were 87 loans recommended amounting to £1,058 ranging from £5 to £32. I had more difficulty in enforcing the proper expenditure of the loans in this county than probably in any other. Before recommending any of the loans I made the closest personal investigation in the locality into every application received, and selected those applicants which required the money most, and were most likely in my mind to turn it to proper account. I could safely have recommended a much larger sum were it available. The selection obliged to be made, out of so many applicants—401—for so small a sum of money, entailed, I need hardly say, a vast amount of time and attention, and could hardly be done without incurring invidious remarks from many who think that, because they have recommended loans, they should be at once made, without reflecting on the vast number of applications for the amount available.

I was obliged to recommend that loans made in 1877, in 12 cases amounting to £156, should be recalled in consequence of the money not having been properly applied. I am quite sure that as much precaution as possible was used in recommending these loans; but it is quite out of our power to insure that in all cases the money will be properly expended. In every case that we can find out that it has not been—and the expenditure of each loan is strictly inquired into—the parties are at once proceeded against for the repayment of the entire loans.

Up to the present I have not been able, from other duties, to investigate the expenditure of the loans made in 1878, except in a few cases, and I am glad to say they have on the whole been satisfactory. I have not been obliged to recommend any loans to be recalled.

The loans proved of great use to the people, and, when fairly expended, have contributed to increased fishing and improved gear.

There were, up to 31st December last, arrears of instalments of loans made in 1875 in one case amounting to £5 5*s.*; out of loans made in 1876, arrears in eight cases amounting to £16 19*s.* 6*d.*; out of loans made in 1877, arrears in one case amounting to £1 0*s.* 9*d.*; none in 1878. Total arrears, £23 5*s.* 3*d.* The total amount issued in this county for the four years was £4,335 10*s.*, out of which there have been repaid £2,558 19*s.* 7*d.*

County Limerick.

The sum available for this county was £625.

There was one application received for a loan of £6, but from the inquiries I made, and the confidential reports received, I could not recommend this to be made, although the most unexceptionable security for the repayment was offered by the applicant.

There are no *bona-fide* fishermen living in this county. Those who follow fishing generally fish for salmon, for which no loans are recommended.

County Clare.

In this county there was available a sum of £343. There were 38 applications received from 55 persons, amounting to £495. Out of these there were 25 loans recommended, amounting to £282, ranging from £5 to £20.

The amount issued was £270. One loan amounting to £12 was cancelled.

I was obliged to recommend loans to be recalled in nine cases out of those made in 1877, amounting to £102, in consequence of the money not having been applied to the purpose for which it was lent. In this county also I experienced great difficulty in enforcing a proper expenditure of the money; but I can with safety say that, except in the cases mentioned above, the several loans have, on the whole, been fairly applied. There were up to 31st December last, arrears of instalments of loans made in 1875, in four cases, amounting to £5 11*s.* 4*d.* Out of loans made in 1876, arrears in one case amounting to £2 2*s.*; out of loans made in 1877, arrears in seven cases, amounting to £17 5*s.* 1*d.* Total arrears, £24 18*s.* 5*d.*

The amount issued in this county for the four years was £1,320, out of which there have been repaid £663 0*s.* 5*d.*

County Kerry.

From that part of the county included in my district there were 15 applications received from 18 persons, amounting to £294 12*s.*, out of which there were 13 loans recommended, amounting to £206. The amount actually issued was £179, the balance of £27, in two loans, having been cancelled for not being taken up in proper time.

I have not been able as yet to investigate the expenditure of the loans made, but this shall be done as speedily as other business will permit.

There are no arrears of instalments in this part of the County Kerry.

General Remarks.

So far, I think the Act of Parliament affording loans to fishermen has proved a success, and an impetus has been given to fishing operations. It is to be regretted that they are not carried out on the west coast on an extensive scale, instead of the uncertain, spasmodic attempts that are made by the poor people living near the coast. This class of persons is unsuitable for large undertakings by themselves, though they might be made useful to others who would enter into the enterprise, which, to command success, must be carried out by the personal superintendence, labour, and active exertions of the principals themselves. Until such people are found, it is well to foster the industry of the poorer classes who now follow fishing on the west coast, and who at seasons are enabled to bring additional supplies of food into the country.

Without the loans, I have no hesitation in saying that many of them would have been obliged to have abandoned fishing long ago. I should like to see the loans extended to the other maritime counties where they are not now available, and where they would be a great boon to many.

I cannot help saying, in conclusion, that I believe much of the arrears of instalments has been caused by inactivity in enforcing repayment, though I would be glad to see indulgence given in really deserving cases. The security taken in each case that has come under my knowledge has been favourably reported on by those from whom I made confidential inquiries, and who were competent to give an opinion. I cannot therefore understand why arrears of instalments should be allowed; one even so far back as August, 1876. On this matter we have felt it our duty to correspond with the Board of Works, who alone are chargeable with the issues and recovery of payments.

I cannot conclude this report without acknowledging the very great and valuable assistance I have received at all times from the country gentlemen and others to whom I have felt it necessary to apply for confidential information on many occasions.

THOS. F. BRADY.

IRISH REPRODUCTIVE LOAN FUND.

MAJOR HAYES' REPORTS FOR THE COUNTY OF CORK AND THAT PART OF THE COUNTY OF KERRY LYING BETWEEN DURSEY ISLAND AND BALLYDAVID HEAD.

COUNTY OF CORK.

Amount available for loans for 1878 was £859. Fifty-eight applications were received, the total sum applied for being £1,872 10s. Of these, seventeen were recommended, one was declined, and sixteen were issued for the full amount available.

All the instalments due up to 31st December, 1877, have been paid.

Of the thirty-six loans recommended in 1876—in twenty-nine the sums lent were expended satisfactorily; two were not expended properly, and were recalled; one was not taken up, and in four cases the expenditure has not been ascertained.

In 1877, of the thirty-two loans recommended for the full amount available, twenty-six were expended satisfactorily, one doubtful, and five not having been so expended have been recommended to be recalled.

In 1878, of the seventeen loans recommended, fourteen have been satisfactorily accounted for, one cancelled, and two not having been expended properly have been recalled.

There are instalments overdue on seven loans, amounting altogether to £36 15s., in four of these cases proceedings have been taken to recover the amounts due, and decrees have been obtained. In the other three the instalments only became due on 1st December last, and will probably be paid in a short time.

This result, after four years in which the Act has been in force, must, I think, be considered very satisfactory.

COUNTY OF KERRY.

Total amount available for 1878 was £2,450. In that part of the county situated in my division one hundred and thirty-seven applications were received, the amount applied for being £3,538. Of these I was able to recommend eighty-seven, for an aggregate sum of £2,261.

In last year's report it was notified that only four instalments of loans, due up to 31st December, 1877, remained unpaid, for a total sum of £13 12*s.* 4*d.*; two of these have since been paid.

Of the nineteen loans made in 1876, seventeen it has been ascertained have been correctly expended, and two, not having been properly spent, have been recalled.

Of the six loans made in 1877, four were properly expended, the other two, although not very satisfactorily accounted for, it was not deemed necessary to recall.

In 1878, eighty-seven loans were recommended; of these forty-five were correctly accounted for, two not quite satisfactorily, and eight were recalled as not properly expended.

One loan was not taken up, twenty-four were issued so late in the year that they have not been yet inquired into, and seven were cancelled from various causes.

Up to the 31st December last, after the Act had been in operation four years, 213 loans have been made for a sum in the aggregate of £5,951. The payments to that date amount to £3,196 9*s.* 7*d.* The instalments in arrears up to the present time number nine, amounting to £36 1*s.* 6*d.* The remainder of the sum issued, however, will not be due for a considerable period.

In the ten cases in arrears prosecutions have been taken in eight, and decrees obtained for the several amounts against the persons in default. The other two only became due on the 1st December last.

I fear that in two cases a loss will accrue, although every precaution was taken before recommending the loans, and the parties were believed to be in every way eligible, and that the loans would be repaid.

MR. BRADY'S REPORT.

ON DIVISION OF IRELAND extending from DUNMORE HEAD, in the county of Kerry, to MULLAGHMORE, in the county of Sligo, embracing in whole or part the counties of Kerry, Clare, Limerick, Tipperary, King's, Queen's, Galway, Longford, Westmeath, Roscommon, Leitrim, Mayo, Cavan, and Sligo.

No. 8, OF LIMERICK DISTRICT.

Extends from Dunmore Head, in the county of Kerry, to Hag's Head, in the county of Clare, and includes all that part of the country the waters of which flow into the sea coast between those points.

The general condition of the salmon fisheries is satisfactory; though the take of fish during the season of 1878 was less productive than that of 1877. No cause can be assigned for the diminished capture. As I have stated in former reports the actual quantity of fish captured during any year cannot be ascertained, there being a reluctance on the part of most proprietors or lessees of fisheries to give any returns, and the public, who preponderate largely in the open waters of this district, will not do so. The average weight of the fish taken has increased very much of late years. This is owing to the protection afforded to the spent fish when descending. A 40 lb. salmon in the Shannon is now of no uncommon occurrence.

The engines fishing in the public waters of the district have again increased in number this year, while there has been at the same time a great increase also in the number of rods. No complaints have been made of the want of fish in the upper waters, though in some places the angling during the year was not good, while in the higher reaches of the Shannon some large captures were made. The highest price obtained for salmon was 1s. 6*d*. per lb., and that for peale or grilse was 1s. The average price for the former was about 1s. 3*d*., and for the latter about 9*d*.

In former reports I entered fully into the capabilities of this district to produce a much larger quantity of salmon than is at present captured, and the wants of the district generally, and to which I beg to refer. Nothing has occurred to alter any of the opinions I therein expressed.

During the past year several inquiries have been held by myself and my colleagues into various matters connected with the district.

Amongst the rest, in consequence of a representation from the Board of Conservators that there was a difficulty in obtaining convictions for breaches of the by-law prohibiting drift nets inside the low water line of ordinary spring tides in Clonderlaw Bay, a public meeting was held at Kilrush to inquire into the subject, but no evidence was offered so as to enable us to make any alteration in the law, even if such were required. We therefore were obliged to dismiss the application and leave it to the Board of Conservators to take the necessary steps to have an adjudication by a competent tribunal on the points in dispute with regard to the by-law—that is, if its provisions have reference to Clonderlaw Bay.

The by-law prohibiting netting in the River Deel or Askeaton has proved of great use. The river is kept exclusively for angling purposes, and, while it forms a most important feeder to the commercial interests of the Shannon, it has amply repaid in sport the proprietors for the interest they have taken and the money they have expended in its improvement. It can be still more improved by some further outlay, and I know of no set of proprietors on a river in Ireland more deserving of support from the public funds of a district than those on the banks of this river. It is seldom that proprietors can be got to expend money on the improvement of rivers, but in this case they have by their exertions made this river in a few years a most important one. They therefore deserve and should obtain from the Board every encouragement to increased exertions.

The case of the mill dam erected on the River Feale, to which I referred fully in former reports as having been raised in height, and now forming a greater obstacle to the passage of fish than the old dam, has been laid before the Law Officers by your Grace's directions, in accordance with our desire. We have been advised that, although the question raised may be very important, it is one more involving local than imperial interests, and calling rather for the expenditure of local than imperial funds. Immediately we caused an urgent representation to be made on the subject to every member of the Board of Conservators, as we considered it to be one of vital importance, not only to the upper water fisheries of the river, but to the large commercial and public interests which at present exist in the tideway; and urged again on the Board our conviction that matters should not be left in this state, but that whatever steps were necessary to enforce compliance with the Act, which required that all dams or other erections in rivers since 1842 should be so built or constructed as to allow of, in one or more places, the free ascent of fish, should be taken before further injury was done to the public fisheries.

The Board of Conservators considered the question at a meeting of their body on the 4th November last, when my colleague, Major Hayes, attended to afford the fullest information on the subject.

The Clerk of the Board was directed to make application to the proprietors and others interested in the fisheries of the river above the mill dam for funds to enable the Board to consider what steps should be taken to require a proper fish pass to be made in the dam. I have since learned that something under £2 was offered to be subscribed. The fact is, the commercial interests in the tidal parts of the river, which are enjoyed by the public, so preponderate over those in the upper waters, that it is hard to expect the upper proprietors to subscribe towards an object from which, even if successful, they may derive, comparatively speaking, little advantage.

The public who fish in the tidal waters are, generally speaking, a poor class of people, and consider they have contributed quite sufficiently towards every object when they have paid the License Duty of £3 on their nets. The Board of Conservators have not the funds at their disposal sufficient for protection alone, without involving themselves in what might turn out to be expensive litigation, the results of which might be uncertain; and they allege further, that the offence of erecting dams in rivers without complying with the provisions of the law in not providing fish passes, is not applicable peculiarly to the Limerick District more than to any other in Ireland; and therefore it would be unjust that their funds alone should be expended in settling a question of law applicable to the whole country. We are strongly of opinion that if the erection of dams in rivers, without sufficient passes for the fish, be permitted with impunity, the public must eventually suffer by the diminished supply of fish. That this was the feeling of the Legislature, when it provided that no dams should be erected after the passing of the Act of 1842, unless there were attached to them such facilities for the free ascent of the fish as would be approved by the Commissioners, there cannot be a doubt; but the omission to provide a penalty for non-compliance with the law, requires, as has been decided, that the proceedings should be by indictment. No private individual or Board of Conservators in Ireland, we believe, will be found to have recourse to this uncertain settlement of an important public question—one which must have a vital effect on the supply of valuable food for the public, and which has been already proved so in the case of most of the rivers in England.

As I stated in a former report, I believe the salmon fisheries of Ireland are at present too valuable a commercial commodity to permit, with impunity, any infraction of the requirements of the statute, because there are no local funds available to put the law in motion. So long as no summary remedy by proceeding for such offences in a similar manner to others is not provided, we are of opinion that the matter should be taken up at the public expense, as being one which affects the public most materially.

In my last and former reports I referred to the practice existing in this district of owners of fixed engines removing them to situations other than those shown on the certificates. The parties were cautioned against a repetition of what were considered offences against the statute. We were advised that the establishment of fixed engines in substantially different situations from those specified in the certificates was an illegal practice; that the proper proceeding was to enforce the penalty under 16th section 32 and 33 V., c. 92, and that, if the justices had any difficulty in convicting, they should be required to state a special case for a Superior Court.

Some of these engines were removed distances varying from a quarter to nearly a mile from the situations specified. The Board of Conservators were remonstrated with against allowing those practices; but they had no funds to justify them in undertaking litigation, particularly as it did not interfere with the general supply, and suggested that it was the province of the Inspectors to hold an inquiry, first summoning the persons before them and issuing an order for the abatement of the engine. The matter was again submitted, and we were advised that the question of law involved could not be properly made the subject of judicial decision by the Inspectors, and that the proper proceeding was by summons before magistrates, and that the Local Board of Conservators, or some individual affected, should be the prosecuting party. The Board have declined doing so. We have no power to compel them.

To allow matters to go on in this way will have the effect of rendering the provisions of the Acts of 1863 and 1868 a nullity, and it becomes our duty to bring the subject now before your Grace.

In my former report I mentioned the very uncertain and unsatisfactory state of the law as regards fixed engines, and to the system allowed by the Board of Conservators of permitting them to be fished for several months without payment of license duty, and to which I beg now to refer.

During the season there were used in this district the following engines:—271 single salmon rods, 43 cross lines, 31 snap nets, 73 draft nets, 137 drift nets, 17 pole nets, 33 stake nets, 1 head weir, 9 boxes or cribs, 133 gaps or eyes for taking eels, producing a total revenue of £2,254 5s., which, though appearing a large sum, is inadequate to the requirements of this large district.

There were 48 water bailiffs during the open, and about 105 during the close season employed by the Conservators, at wages ranging from 5s. to £1 per week. Only a few employed by private individuals, and these only to watch trespassers.

During the year there were 110 prosecutions by the Conservators, and 95 convictions obtained; by the Constabulary and others, with the assistance of the secretary of the Conservators, 29, of which 21 were convicted. Offences against the fishery laws appear not to have increased, while there is no perceptible diminution.

The close seasons in this district are—For tidal and fresh waters:—

"Between 31st July and 12th February, save rivers Cashen and Tributaries, and save between Kerry Head and Dunmore Head, and Loop Head and Hag's Head, and all rivers running into the sea between those points.

"For Cashen down to its mouth and Tributaries, between 31st August and 1st June; between Dunmore Head and Kerry Head, and all rivers flowing into the sea between those points, between 15th September and 1st April; between Loop Head and Hag's Head, and all rivers running into the sea between those points, between 15th September and 1st May."

For angling with single rods and lines:—

"Between 30th September and 1st February, save Cashen and Maigue rivers and their Tributaries; and save all rivers running into the sea between Loop Head and Hag's Head, and between Dunmore Head and Kerry Head. For Cashen and Tributaries, between 31st October and 16th March; for Maigue and Tributaries, between 30th September and 20th February; between Loop Head and Hag's Head, between 30th September and 1st March, and between Dunmore Head and Kerry Head, between 30th September and 1st April."

The bye-laws in force in the district are as follows:—

In River Shannon:—

"Prohibiting net fishing in that part of the River Shannon between Wellesley-bridge and the Railway bridge, between 1st June and 12th February.

"Prohibiting between the 1st day of August, or such other day as may be the first day of the close season, and the 1st day of November in each year, the use of draft nets, or any other net or nets used as a draft net, having a foot-rope and leads or weights affixed thereto, within the following limits, viz.:—In that part of the River Shannon situate between the Fishing weir known as the Lax Weir, and a line drawn due north and south across the said River Shannon at the western extremity of Graigue Island.

"Prohibiting draft nets for the capture of fish of any kind, of a mesh less than one and three-quarter inches from knot to knot, to be measured along the side of the square, or seven inches to be measured all round each such mesh, such measurements being taken in the clear when the net is wet, in the tidal parts of the River Shannon, or in the tidal parts of any of the rivers flowing into the said River Shannon.

"Prohibiting the fishing for salmon or trout by any means whatsoever, within a space of twenty yards from the weir wall of Tarmonbarry, on the River Shannon.

"Prohibiting having nets for capture of salmon or trout on board any cot or curragh between mouth of Shannon and Wellesley-bridge, in the city of Limerick, or in tidal parts of any rivers flowing into the said River Shannon between said points, between the hours of nine o'clock on Saturday morning and three o'clock on Monday morning; or between Wellesley-bridge and the Navigation Weir at Killaloe, in the county of Clare, between eight o'clock on Saturday morning and four o'clock on Monday morning.

"Prohibiting the shooting of fish in that part of River Shannon between Portumna-bridge and Shannon-bridge."

In River Shannon and Clonderlaw Bay:—

"Regulating the use of drift nets as follows:—

"First.—That no drift nets of greater length than 100 yards shall be used for the capture of salmon or trout in any part of the River Shannon between Limerick and a line drawn across the river below Askeaton, from Aughnish Point, in the county of Limerick, to Kildysart, in the county of Clare.

"Second.—That no drift nets of greater length than 200 yards shall be used for the capture of salmon or trout in any other tidal waters of the River Shannon, or in Clonderlaw Bay.

"Third.—That no two or more drift nets shall be attached together in any way or be allowed to drift within 150 yards of each other in the River Shannon, or in Clonderlaw Bay.

"Fourth.—That no drift nets below, or seaward of a line drawn across the River Shannon, from Aughnish Point, in the county of Limerick, to Kildysart, in the county of Clare, shall be used within the line of low-water mark of ordinary spring tides.

"Fifth.—That no drift nets shall be used in Clonderlaw Bay above a line drawn from Knock to Lacknabahee, in the county of Clare.

"That no drift nets shall be used in the Rivers Maigue or Askeaton."

In Lough Ree :—

"Permitting the use of nets, having a mesh of five inches in the round, measured when the net is wet."

In River Fergus :—

"Prohibiting the fishing for salmon or trout by any means whatsoever, within a space of twenty yards from the weir wall of Ennis.

"Prohibiting the use of drift nets in the tidal parts of River."

In River Maigue :—

"Prohibiting the use of draft nets between Ferry Drawbridge and the old bridge of Adare.

"Prohibiting use of all nets, except landing nets as auxiliary to rod and line, above Railway bridge below Adare.

"Prohibiting the use of drift nets.

"Prohibiting the shooting of fish."

In Lough Derg :—

"Permitting the use of nets not exceeding twelve yards in length, with meshes of one inch from knot to knot, for the capture of fish other than salmon and trout.

"Prohibiting the use of nets (except landing nets as auxiliary to angling with rod and line) for the capture of fish other than eels, between eight o'clock in the evening and six o'clock in the morning."

In River Deel or Askeaton :—

"Prohibiting the use of drift nets.

"Prohibiting the use of all nets (except landing nets as auxiliary to angling with rod and line) for the capture of salmon or trout in that part of the river situate between Broken Bridge and the mouth of River as defined."

The principal Rivers in the Limerick District, and their seasons for Netting and Angling for Salmon and Trout, are as follows :—

Rivers.	Tidal Netting.	Freshwater Netting, &c.	Angling, Single Rod and Line.
Carben,	1st June to 31st August, inclusive,	Same as Tidal,	16th March to 31st Oct., inclusive.
Clohane,	1st April to 15th Sept., do.,	do.,	1st April to 30th Sept., do.
Deel or Askeaton,	Not allowed,	do.,	1st February to 30th Sept., do.
Doonbeg,	1st May to 15th Sept., do.,	do.,	1st May to 30th Sept., do.
Ennistimon or Lahinch,	Do. do.,	do.,	Do. do.
Fergus,	12th Feb. to 31st July, do.,	do.,	1st February to 30th Sept., do.
Maigue,	Do. do.,	do.,	20th February to 30th Sept., do.
Shannon,	Do. do.,	do.,	1st February to 30th Sept., do.

9, or Galway District,

Extends from Hag's Head, in the county Clare, to Slyne Head, in the county Galway, and includes all that part of the country the waters of which flow into the coast between those two points.

The take of fish has been less in 1878 than former year. Nothing could more clearly show the difficulty of accounting for the decreased capture of fish than this district. Here the fish may be seen, I may say, in thousands any day in summer when the water is sufficiently low. There are no disturbing influences such as exist in other places to diminish the supply. There are no fixed engines within 100 miles of the river. There is a large free gap in the fishing weirs in the river. The proprietors in the tidal waters expend a large sum of money annually on protection, and everything appears to be well managed. There appears to be a very large supply of fish in the upper waters, and, so far as I could learn, except in a few places, they are well protected, and yet, notwithstanding all, the supply fell short. It is said that fish are running later than usual, and that large quantities are seen ascending after the close season has commenced.

The angling was about equal to that of 1877, which was the best, save one year, for the past eighteen years.

It is very difficult to account for this falling off. I have always stated that there will be fluctuations in salmon fisheries no matter what care is bestowed on them; and I cannot have a better illustration of the correctness of this view than the rivers in this district.

The foregoing observations refer to almost every river in it, but there are in some rivers some additional reasons for increasing capture instead of a falling off, which I think well to mention.

In the Ballinahinch river, after a jubilee of two years free from netting, it was naturally expected that there would have been an enormously increased quantity of fish in the third year, which would amply repay not only the commercial but the sporting interests. Netting was resumed last year, but not to the full extent, and I was informed it hardly paid its expenses, while the angling had not improved.

In the Screeb and other rivers no netting has been allowed for several years, and yet the angling was bad.

About 30 water-bailiffs employed by the Conservators in this district, half all the year round, the others from one to three months, at salaries of from £2 to £10. There are about 230 employed by private individuals, the majority of them by the lessees of the tidal fisheries.

The highest price obtained for salmon in this district during the year was 2*s.* 6*d.* per lb.; the lowest, 8*d.* There has been an increase in the size of the fish captured—the average weight of salmon being over 15 lbs., and that of peale or grilse over 6 lbs. There have been no cases of poisoning during the year, and offences against the fishery laws have diminished. There were 18 prosecutions by the Conservators, and two by the constabulary during the year—convictions in all the cases.

During the season the following engines were used in the district:—147 single salmon rods; 9 cross lines and rods; 12 draft nets; 6 trammel nets; 4 boxes or cribs; 21 gaps or eyes for taking eels; producing a revenue of £271.

The close seasons in force in the district are as follows:—

For tidal and upper waters:—

"Between 15th August and 1st February."

For angling with single rod and line:—

"Between 15th October and 1st February, save in Cashla, Doohulla, Spiddal, Ballinahinch, Crumlin, Screeb, and Inver rivers, which is between 31st October and 1st February."

The bye-laws in force are:—

In Galway River, and Loughs Corrib and Mask, and Tributaries:—

"Prohibiting the use of the instrument commonly called strokehawl or snatch, or any other such instrument.

"Prohibiting the use of nets of any kind whatsoever in any part of the rivers known as the Clare and Claregalway or Turloughmore rivers, in the county of Galway, above the junction of said rivers with Lough Corrib.

"Prohibiting the snatching or attempting to snatch salmon in any tidal or fresh waters in the district with any kind of fish hook covered in part or in whole with any matter or thing, or uncovered."

Rivers.	Tidal Netting.	Freshwater Netting, &c.	Angling with Single Rod and Line.
Ballinahinch,	1st Feb. to 15th August, inclusive,	Same as Tidal,	1st Feb. to 31st October, inclusive.
Cashla,	Do. do.,	do.,	Do. do.
Crumlin,	Do. do.,	do.,	Do. do.
Doohulla,	Do. do.,	do.,	Do. do.
Galway,	Do. do.,	do.,	1st Feb. to 15th October, do.
Inver,	Do. do.,	do.,	1st Feb. to 31st October, do.
Kilcolgan,	Do. do.,	do.,	1st Feb. to 15th October, do.
Spiddle,	Do. do.,	do.,	1st Feb. to 31st October, do.
Screeb,	Do. do.,	do.,	Do. do.

10¹, Ballynakill District,

Extends from Slyne Head, co. Galway, to Pidgeon Point, co. Mayo, and includes all that part of the country the waters of which flow into the coast between those two points.

The take of fish in this district during the past year has been also much less than in the preceding one. No reason can be assigned.

The amount of protection is much the same as former years. The quantity of breeding fish observed in the rivers is reported to be less than in preceding year. The spring salmon taken has increased in their average weight—average, 14 to 18 lbs.; that of peale, 5 to 7 lbs. They are nearly all exported.

Offences against the fishery laws have diminished. There were only 7 prosecutions by the Conservators during the year. Some of the proprietors employ private water-bailiffs, but only to a small extent. One proprietor subscribed £32 10*s.* towards protection.

The following engines were used in the district in 1878, viz.:—53 single salmon rods; 17 draft nets; 1 drift net; 2 pole nets; producing a total revenue of £111—a sum far short of the actually necessary requirements of the district.

There are no pollutions flowing into any of the rivers poisonous to fish.

The close seasons in force are as follows :—

In tidal and fresh waters :—

"Between 31st August and 16th February, save in Louisburgh and Carrowniskey rivers and estuaries, which is between 15th September and 1st July."

For angling with single rod :—

"Between 31st October and 1st February, save in Louisburgh and Carrowniskey rivers, which is between 31st October and 1st July."

There are no special by-laws in the district.

The principal rivers in the Ballinakill District, and the seasons for Netting and Angling for Salmon or Trout, are as follows :—

Rivers.	Tidal Netting.	Freshwater Netting	Angling with Single Rod and Line.
Carrowniskey, .	1st July to 15th Sept., inclusive, .	Same as Tidal, .	1st July to 31st October, inclusive.
Clifden, . .	10th Feb. to 31st Aug., do., .	do., .	1st Feb. to 31st October, do.
Delphi, . .	Do. do., .	do., .	Do. do.
Dawros or Kylemore, . .	Do. do., .	do., .	Do. do.
Erriff, . . .	Do. do., .	do., .	Do. do.
Louisburgh, .	1st July to 15th Sept., do., .	do., .	1st July to 31st October, do.

10°, or Bangor District,

Extends from Pidgeon Point, co. Mayo has to Benwee Head, and includes all that part of the country the waters of which flow into the coast between those two points.

In this district also the take of fish in 1878 has very much fallen off, and cannot be accounted for. It is reported that the same amount of protection has been afforded as in former years, but there have been no prosecutions by either the Conservators or the Constabulary, and offences against the fishery laws are diminished. From this district emanated the loudest complaints of poaching and lawlessness on the part of the country people. If such an improvement has taken place that there was during a whole year no necessity for prosecutions, a more prosperous state of things than that now reported as to the quantity of fish taken may be hopefully looked forward to.

The number of bailiffs employed by the Conservators was 75, and about 27 by private individuals, chiefly in the open season. No contributions towards the funds are received by the Conservators from any upper proprietors, but in some rivers the lessees of the tidal waters supplement the funds for the purpose of protection in the close season.

The appeal against the order altering the definition of the estuary of the Owenmore and Owenduff rivers was heard during the year, and allowed by the Judicial Committee of the Privy Council before which it came. As the merits of the question were not entered into, a further application has been received to alter the definition made by our predecessors, and it will form the subject of inquiry during the year.

The following engines were used in 1878 :—31 single salmon rods ; 25 draft nets, and 12 bag nets ; producing a revenue of £225.

The close seasons in the district are as follows :—

For tidal and fresh waters :—

"Between the 31st August and 16th February, save in Newport, Glenamoy, Burrishoole, and Owengarve Rivers and Estuaries ; for Newport River and Estuary, 31st August and 20th March ; for Glenamoy River and Estuary, 15th September and 1st May ; for Burrishoole and Owengarve and Estuaries 31st August and 16th February."

For angling with single rod and line :—

"Between 30th September and 1st May, save Burrishoole between 31st October and 1st February, Newport between 30th September and 1st May, Owengarve and Glenamoy between 31st October and 1st May, Owenmore and Munhim between 30th September and 1st February, Owenduff or Ballycroy, and Ballyveeny and Owenduff, and all rivers in Achill Island, between 31st October and 1st February."

The bye-laws in force in this district are as follows :—

"Prohibiting the removal of gravel or sand from any part of the bed of the Owenmore River, in the County of Mayo, where the spawning of Salmon or Trout may take place.

"Permitting the use of Nets with Meshes of one and a half inches from knot to knot (to be measured along the side of the square, or six inches to be measured all round each such Mesh, such measurements being taken in the clear, when the Net is wet), within so much of the said Rivers Owenduff or Ballycroy, Owenmore and Munhim, as lies above the mouth as defined, during so much of the months of June, July, and August, as do now or at any time may form part of the Open Season for the capture of Salmon or Trout with Nets, in the said Rivers."

The following are the principal Rivers in the Bangor District, with the Seasons for Netting and Angling for Salmon and Trout :—

Rivers.	Tidal Netting.	Fresh Netting.	Angling with Single Rod and Line
Achill Island, .	16th Feb. to 31st Aug., inclusive,	Same as Tidal, .	1st Feb. to 31st October, inclusive.
Ballycroy, . .	Do. do., .	do., .	Do. do.
Burrishoole, .	Do. do., .	do., .	Do. do.
Glenamoy, . .	1st May to 15th Sept., do., .	do., .	1st May to 31st October, do.
Moyour, . .	16th Feb. to 31st Aug., do., .	do., .	1st May to 30th Sept., do.
Munhim, . .	Do. do., .	do., .	1st Feb. to 30th Sept., do.
Newport, . .	20th March to 31st Aug., do., .	do., .	1st May to 30th Sept., do.
Owenmore, . .	16th Feb. to 31st Aug., do., .	do., .	1st Feb. to 30th Sept., do.
Owengarve, . .	Do. do., .	do., .	1st May to 31st October, do.

11, or Ballina District,

Extends from Benwee Head, in the county of Mayo, to Coonamore Point, in the county of Sligo, and includes all that part of the country the waters of which flow into the coast between those two points.

No district in Ireland is managed with more efficiency towards protection and the full development of the salmon fisheries than this district. Nearly £1,000 a year is annually expended on this alone, and the great bulk of this sum is contributed by the proprietors of the Tidal Fisheries of the River Moy, by whom I have been favoured with a return of the amount expended and the number of bailiffs employed by them since the year 1866 to the present date—which averages £827, and about 300 bailiffs annually. The proprietor of the fisheries in the Easkey River also expends a considerable sum in the protection of that river. The take of fish in the lower or tidal fisheries during 1878 was notwithstanding all this care much less than in 1877. The cause for this cannot be assigned.

It is alleged that the great number of drift nets in the bay, and the manner in which they are fished, has the effect of breaking the schools of fish and driving them out to sea. This does not exist in Galway where the fisheries are also well managed and where there was a like failure in the catch—so that it is hard to say if this allegation is correct. There is, however, one fact worth noticing that, since the great increase in the number of those engines fishing, the quantity of fish captured by the bag nets which are set on both sides of the bay has so fallen off that they are hardly worth fishing, for some years barely covering the expense. In former reports I alluded to the manner in which these drift nets were used in this bay and which I believed to be perfectly illegal. The tests therein referred to have since been applied, and through the kindness of the Captain commanding the guardship of the district we were enabled to have the assistance of two Coastguard Officers to carry out the experiment of remaining with their nets all night while fishing. It was stated by some of the people who use these nets, but who are not *bona fide* fishermen, that it would be impossible for them to do so without great danger and risk. We placed a Coastguard Officer in each of two of the fishing boats of the locality, with the ordinary fishing crew, and they were enabled to stop out at the fishing every night during the past season. They were each supplied with books to make a full report of everything and to keep observations, and their journals will aid us most materially in coming to some satisfactory settlement of this most vexed question.

I think it is only due to the officers who were lent to us for this service, which was a most onerous one, and against whom intimidations of rather a violent character were at first used, that they discharged it with energy, independence, great caution, and to the entire satisfaction of the Inspectors. The names of the officers to whom was entrusted this duty are—Mr. Richard G. Jagoe, Chief Boatman in charge Coastguard Station, Ballyvaughan, county Clare, and Mr. George M'Kinley, Chief Boatman in charge at Barna, county Galway—both of whom had on previous occasions carried out experiments relative to trawling in Galway Bay.

During the last fishing season it was determined that we should ourselves ascertain whether these nets were legally fished, or were, as had been frequently alleged, used as fixed nets by having heavy weights attached to them. The Captain commanding the guardship having very kindly placed at our disposal for the purpose, Her Majesty's Cutter *Victoria*, I proceeded therein to the bay quite unknown to the fishermen, and came in at night when only the nets are set, and felt it my duty to make, with the assistance of the cutter's men, several seizures of nets illegally fixed. All the parties were afterwards prosecuted to conviction, and their nets forfeited and sold. It was not at all unlikely that in performing this most unpleasant duty serious consequences might have arisen amongst the fishermen who showed a determination at first to resist all authority, but for the judicious conduct and energy of Mr. James Coleman, the officer of the cutter, to whom was entrusted this duty and who discharged it fearlessly but temperately and to my entire satisfaction. The fishermen have all been cautioned against a repetition of these offences, and warned that similar steps will be taken next season to enforce the law. The Bye-Laws applied for regulating this mode of fishing will receive immediate consideration.

With the exception of the cases mentioned I do not know of any proprietor of fisheries in this important district, expending any money for the protection of the fisheries; although in the river Moy, since the opening of the Free Gap in the fishing weir, valuable commercial fisheries have been created for the upper proprietors.

Before the Legislation of 1863 there was but one fishery in this river where netting was carried on. There are now in the distance of about 13 miles no fewer than 20 nets used, and the quantity of salmon taken last season in that space was one-third greater than that taken in the extensive tidal fisheries of the estuary and the bay. On this subject I beg to refer to former reports. So long as the upper proprietors had no, or very little interest in the fisheries by reason of the fishing weirs without a free gap barring the ascent of fish to their waters, except during the weekly close season, it could not be expected they would contribute towards the expense of protection. But since all this has been removed, and the fish have a free escape to the upper waters, where valuable properties, from which large revenues are derived since 1864, have been created, it was not too much to expect that funds would be contributed by the proprietors towards maintaining and increasing this property.

With the exception, however, of the License Duty, on the nets used, which it is imperative on the lessees of these fisheries to pay, I do not know a single instance where any assistance is afforded by the upper proprietors. All is left to the proprietors of the tidal fisheries who have so large an interest that they are forced, in defence of their property, to make great sacrifices to maintain it. Were the fisheries in the tidal waters public or divided amongst a number of proprietors as in the upper waters, the fisheries of the river would, without doubt, be most materially injured, and the public would eventually be the sufferers. I cannot think that such a course as I have pointed out is at all equitable.

There were 62 prosecutions by the Conservators during the year. Offences against the Fishery Laws have diminished.

Angling is prohibited in this district during the descent of the fry, so that little or no destruction takes place by it.

The following engines have been used in the district in 1878, viz.:—75 salmon rods, 40 draft nets, 51 drift nets, 5 bag nets, 7 boxes or cribs, and 13 eyes or gaps for taking eels, producing a revenue of £451, which would be completely inadequate for protection but for the large sums expended by the owners of the fisheries in the tidal waters.

For tidal waters the close seasons in force are:—Netting, between 12th August and 16th March, save Palmerston and Easkey Rivers, which is between 31st August and 1st June.

For upper waters—Netting, between 31st July and 1st February, save Palmerston and Easkey Rivers, which is between 31st August and 1st June. Angling—Between 15th September and 1st February, save Easkey river and tributaries, which is between 30th September and 1st June, and save Cloonaghmore or Palmerston River and tributaries: the tidal parts being between 31st October and 1st February, and upper parts being between 31st October and 1st June.

The bye-laws in force are as follows:—

"Permitting use of nets with meshes of one and a quarter inches from knot to knot to be measured along the side of the square, or five inches to be measured all round each such mesh, such measurements being taken in the clear, when the net is wet.

"Prohibiting angling for trout during April and May in each year—Loughs Conn and Cullen excepted."

The principal rivers in the Ballina district and the seasons for netting and angling for salmon or trout are as follow:—

Rivers.	Tidal Netting	Freshwater Netting.	Angling with Single Rod and Line.
Ballycastle, . .	16th Mar. to 12th Aug., inclusive.	1 Feb. & 31 July	1st Feb. to 15th Sept. inclusive.
Cloonaghmore or Palmerston,	1st June to 31st Aug. do. .	Same as Tidal, .	In tidal water, 1st Feb. to 31st Oct., and in up waters, 1st June to 31st Oct. inclusive.
Easkey, . .	1st June to 31st Aug. do. .	do.	1st June to 30th Sept. inclusive.
Moy, . . .	16th Mar. to 12th Aug. do. .	1 Feb. & 31 July	1st Feb. to 15th Sept. inclusive.

12, or Sligo District,

Extends from Coonamore Point, County Sligo, to Mullaghmore Point, and includes that part of the country the waters of which flow into the coast between those two points.

The general state of the salmon fisheries in the district is reported as favourable, though the take of summer fish or grilse was less than in preceding year. The take of salmon was about the same. The spring fish is getting larger every year; they average now about 13 lbs. The amount of protection by the Conservators was about the same as former years. The Bailiffs heretofore employed by the Proprietors of the Tidal Fisheries were not, it is reported, re-appointed during the last season. This is stated to be in consequence of the alteration in the open season, which cut off 15 days of their early and best fishing, viz.:—from the 1st to the 15th January inclusive.

Whether the angling has improved in consequence I could not obtain any authentic information.

The quantity of breeding fish has increased. It is reported that offences against the Fishery Laws are about the same as former years. However there were no prosecutions during the year by the Conservators.

The engines used during the year were:—14 salmon rods; 1 cross line; 19 draft nets; 1 bag net; 5 gap or eyes for eels; producing a revenue of £87, which is wholly inadequate for the necessary protection.

The close seasons in force are—for tidal waters—

"Between 19th August and 4th February, save Sligo river and Estuary, which is between 31st July and 16th January."

For fresh waters—

"Between 19th August and 4th February, save Sligo river which is between 31st July and 16th January."

For angling with single rod—

"Between 30th September and 1st February, save in Drumcliffe river and Glencar lake between 19th October and 1st February."

The bye-laws in force are as follows:—

"Prohibiting the snatching, or attempting to snatch, salmon in Sligo river with any kind of fish-hook, covered in part or in whole, or uncovered.

"Permitting use of nets with meshes of half an inch from knot to knot, for capture of fish."

The principal rivers in the Sligo district and the seasons for netting and angling for salmon or trout are as follows:—

Rivers.	Tidal Netting	Freshwater Netting.	Angling with Single Rod and Line.
Ballisodare, . .	4th Feb. to 19th Aug. inclusive, .	Same as Tidal,	1st Feb. to 30th Sept. inclusive.
Drumcliffe, . .	do.	do. .	1st Feb. to 19th Oct. do.
Grange, . . .	do	do. .	1st Feb. to 30th Sept. do.
Sligo, . . .	16th Jan. to 31st July inclusive, .	do. .	do. do.

In conclusion I have only to say that although the Salmon Fisheries of Ireland on the whole, during the past year, have partly partaken of the general decline in capture which occurred in other countries, I believe them to be in a satisfactory condition, but that there will always occur a fluctuation in the produce over which man has, up to the present, no control, or little knowledge to prevent, I have no doubt.

The Coastguard and Constabulary have been most active as a general rule in giving assistance in the enforcement of the laws, and I have invariably found from both services the most cordial assistance, cheerfully and earnestly given, whenever required.

THOMAS F. BRADY.

MAJOR HAYES' REPORT.

Division extending from SLEA HEAD in the County of KERRY in the west to WICKLOW HEAD in the east, and including eight fishery districts—viz., No. 7, KILLARNEY; No. 6², KENMARE; No. 6², BANTRY; No. 6¹, SKIBBEREEN; No. 5, CORK; No. 4, LISMORE; No. 3, WATERFORD; and No. 2, WEXFORD, which embrace the whole or portions of the following counties, viz. :—KERRY, CORK, WATERFORD, TIPPERARY, LIMERICK, KILKENNY, CARLOW, WEXFORD, QUEEN'S COUNTY, KING'S COUNTY, KILDARE, and Wicklow.

No. 7. KILLARNEY DISTRICT.

Extending from Lamb Head to Dunmore Head, both in the county of Kerry.

The capture of salmon in this district was considerably below that of 1877. The season commenced well, and gave promise of being very abundant, but as the Summer advanced it fell off, and resulted unsatisfactorily.

The continued severe frosts, commencing in November, prevented the fish in the spawning season finding their way into the smaller streams, and it is reported that the quantity of breeding fish seen was less than in the previous year.

The average size of the salmon and peale has increased considerably.

In 1876 salmon averaged 10 lbs. weight.
" peale " 5 "
In 1878 salmon " 12 "
" peale " 6 "

Preservation is looked after in this district by private owners of fisheries more vigorously than in most others. In addition to 80 Water Bailiffs employed by the Board of Conservators, some 40 are employed by individual proprietors.

It is gratifying to find that no cases of poisoning rivers occurred during the year, a very unusual fact in this District.

Offences against the Fishery Laws about the same in 1878 as in 1877.

There were 48 prosecutions, resulting in 32 convictions, and 16 cases in which the summonses were dismissed. Of the 32 convictions 4 were subsequently reversed on appeal to Quarter Sessions, it is believed in consequence of the summonses not having been taken out under proper sections of the Acts of Parliament.

The table of close seasons and the Bye-laws in force in this district will be found at pp. 65 and 68.

The following engines were licensed in this district in 1878 :—102 salmon rods, 4 cross lines, 64 draft nets, 2 boxes or cribs, producing with the amount received upon the percentage on Poor Law Valuation and fines inflicted, a total of £403 1s. available for protection, as against £405 5s. for the year 1877.

I do not regard the unsatisfactory season of 1878 as an indication of decline in the fisheries of this district, but rather as the result of an exceptionally unsuitable condition of weather during the fishing season.

No. 6³. KENMARE DISTRICT.

Extending from Crow Head to Lamb Head, in the county of Kerry.

The reports received from the Kenmare district for 1878 are satisfactory. It is officially reported that the sweeper nets captured more fish than in the preceding year.

In this as in the Killarney district individual proprietors do much to secure proper preservation, by employing Water Bailiffs at their own expense, independently of those paid out of public funds by the Conservators.

The state of the spawning beds in regard to the stock of fish seen upon them in the season, was very satisfactory.

No observable change in the size of the fish has been remarked.

Offences against the Fishery Laws are reported as having diminished considerably, and there was only one instance of poisoning during the year—this was on the Roughty River.

In consequence of an application that we should inquire into the system of netting with sweep nets carried on in the Kenmare Estuary, and the allegation that the system pursued was detrimental to the fisheries, the Inspectors issued notices that a public meeting would be held to inquire into the subjects at Kenmare, on the 18th October last.

The inquiry was held, and evidence taken on the subject, the result of which was that, in the interest of the fisheries, we deemed it necessary to make a Bye-law containing the following clauses :—

"1. It is prohibited, and it is hereby prohibited to use any Net for the capture of salmon or trout in any part of the said Kenmare River or Bay of greater length than One Hundred and Thirty Yards.

"2. It is prohibited, and it is hereby prohibited to beat the water or to throw stones or other missiles therein during the time of shooting or drafting Nets for the capture of salmon or trout in the said Kenmare River or Bay.

"Each and every person offending against any of these Bye-Laws, Rules, and Regulations, shall forfeit and pay for each offence a sum of FIVE POUNDS, and every Net used contrary hereto shall be forfeited."

The Bye-law is now progressing through the different stages required by Act of Parliament. When these are completed it will be submitted to Your Grace and Privy Council for approval.

It is believed that this Bye-law will have a very beneficial effect upon the fisheries of the Kenmare District.

The engines licensed and used in 1878 were 22 single rods, 7 draft nets, 5 sweepers and 1 bag net, producing altogether £57 10s., which, with £6, the per-centage on Poor Law Valuation, amounted to £63 10s., as compared with £76 5s. available for protection.

For table of close seasons see page 68 of Appendix.

Mr. Mahony, of Dromore Castle, still continues his operations in artificial propagation of salmon, and there is little doubt but his efforts have done much to secure the stock of fish being kept up as it has hitherto been.

No. 6[2]. BANTRY DISTRICT.

Extending from Mizen Head to Crow Head, in the county of Cork.

It is reported that the capture of salmon in 1878 was less than in the preceding year.

The stock of fish, however, on the spawning beds was greater.

The average size of the fish about the same as last year.

Only two offences against the Fishery Laws were the subject of prosecution ; in both cases the parties were convicted.

The Bye-laws affecting this district will be found at page 65 of Appendix, and the close season table at page 68.

Licensed engines in use in 1878—13 salmon rods and 12 draft nets, which, with amount received for fines, &c., produced a revenue available for protection of £53 13s. 7d., as compared with £48 in 1877.

No. 6[1]. SKIBBEREEN DISTRICT.

Extending from Galley Head to Mizen Head in the County of Cork.

The report of the produce of this district is again unsatisfactory—the report being that the capture was much less in 1878 than in 1877.

The stock of fish on the spawning beds is also reported as less.

In last year's Report it was stated that, "in consequence of applications from the Board of Conservators of the district, inquiries will be held, as soon as other engagements will permit, into the different subjects of complaint, &c."

In conformity with the foregoing a public meeting was held at Skibbereen, on the 9th May last, and the following subjects were inquired into :—

1. As to close seasons.
2. Definition of mouths of rivers.
3. Prohibition of drift nets.
4. To repeal Bye-law permitting the capture of salmon by nets with meshes of one inch from knot to knot.

The inquiries resulted in our making the following changes :—

1. As regards close season—

For nets and all other engines in Tidal Waters, save single rods and lines—Close season to commence on 15th September instead of 30th, and to end on 1st May.

Fresh Waters—To commence on 1st August instead of 30th September, and end on 1st May.

No change *in season* for single rods and lines.

2. As to definition of mouths of rivers—

After careful inquiry we considered it necessary to re-define the mouth of the principal river in the district, the Ilen, as shown upon a map attached to the order, and which is now awaiting the approval of Your Grace and Privy Council.

With regard to the other rivers in the district, we came to the conclusion that no change was necessary.

3. As to drift nets—

The decision at which we arrived was, that drift nets, fished in such narrow waters as those in this district, were most injurious.

A Bye-law prohibiting their use was accordingly prepared, and this is also awaiting approval.

4. On the subject of repealing the Bye-laws permitting the use of small-mesh nets—

The question was deferred for another year, as it was considered that the Bye-law should have further trial, before any decision could properly be arrived at, with regard to the necessity for repealing it.

For Bye-laws and Close season tables see pp. 65 and 68 of appendix.

The following engines were licensed in 1878—15 draft nets and 11 single rods, producing together £56, which, with £2 14*s.* received on account of fines for offences against the Fishery Laws, amounted to £58 14*s.*, available for protection, as against £62 14*s.* 4*d.* in 1877.

No. 5. Cork District

Extending from Ballycotton Head to Galley Head, both in the county of Cork.

I am again in a position to report favourably of this district, both net and rod fishings having been most prosperous, and the capture much greater in 1878 than in the previous year.

For several years this improvement has been steadily going on, and is mainly due to the great interest taken in the fisheries by the Board of Conservators, and also to the action of the Cork Anglers' Club, which is still pursuing its steady course of usefulness, in aiding in the preservation of the rivers.

The Bye-laws which I referred to in my last report, prohibiting the use of drift nets in the River Lee and estuary, and prohibiting the keeping of salmon nets on board boats during the weekly close time, have been found most salutary; and there can be no doubt have tended to the improvement of the fisheries; but it is exceedingly difficult to devise measures which will prove thoroughly effective in putting down poaching, where the habit has been long established, and when it is attended with considerable profit.

Thus in the case of the Bye-law prohibiting the use of drift nets in the Lee and Estuary, it was found that some of the owners of these nets have since had them licensed as draft nets, using them openly as such, but at night and when not closely watched by the Bailiffs some were fished in the ordinary way as drift nets. The result was that in the early part of the season a great proportion of the fish taken was captured by the drifts. This was clearly seen, from the marks upon the fish when exhibited for sale in the markets.

A further inquiry was in consequence held into the matter, and it was shown to our satisfaction that the only way to meet the difficulty was to make a Bye-law regulating the maximum size of the meshes of nets to be used for the capture of salmon in the River Lee.

This was accordingly done, and the following bye-law was prepared, and having been since approved by Your Grace and the Privy Council of Ireland, it is now in force. The maximum limit of mesh to ten inches, it is believed, will secure that the nets used will practically be useless as drift nets, as few salmon can mesh in them :—

"Whereas the practice of using nets, having meshes of greater dimensions than two and one-half inches from knot to knot, or ten inches in the round, in any tidal waters in that part of the district heretofore defined and known as No. 5, or "The Cork District," situated inside or to the northward of a straight line drawn in the direction of Templebreedy Church, from the Lighthouse at Roche's Point on the east, to the Mainland on the west, all in the county of Cork, is in our opinion detrimental to the fisheries of the said district, and it seems to Us, the Inspectors of Irish Fisheries, to be expedient for the more effectual government, management, protection, and improvement of the salmon and trout fisheries in the said district, to prohibit such practice, and to impose and prescribe conditions and restrictions as to the size of the meshes thereof; Now, We, the said Inspectors, acting under the powers and authorities given to us, do make and ordain this Bye-law, by which it is prohibited, and it is hereby prohibited to use any net for the capture of salmon or trout in any part of the aforesaid tidal waters of said district having meshes of greater dimensions than two and one-half inches from knot to knot, to be measured along the side of the square, or ten inches to be measured all round each such mesh, such measurements being taken in the clear when the net is wet.

"Each and every person offending against this Bye-law shall forfeit and pay for each offence a sum of Five Pounds, and every net having meshes of greater dimensions than aforesaid, and found in any of the places in which it is hereby prohibited to use such net, shall be forfeited."

The stock of fish on the spawning grounds is reported as greater than in 1877.

The average size of salmon, 12 to 14 lbs.

The rod fishings are steadily and largely increasing in value, and the success attending the rod fishers has been very gratifying—from four or five, to ten or twelve salmon, having been not an out-of-the-way capture in a single day to one rod.

Had this desirable result heen obtained by any sacrifice of the net fishery interests, it would not have heen satisfactory, but this has not been so. The nets also have been most successful, and have contributed a considerably increased supply of fish to the markets.

For Close season tables and the Bye-laws in force in the district, see pp. 64, 65, and 68 of Appendix.

With the approval of the authorities a gunboat was again stationed on the Lee to aid in preservation during the past Close season. Her services were most valuable, a number of nets illegally fishing having been seized by her crew

Offences against the Fishery Laws are reported as having diminished.

Fifty-one cases of prosecution occurred. Of these, the parties in forty were convicted and fined, and eleven were dismissed.

The following engines were licensed and fished during the season 1878 :—283 single rods, 8 cross lines, 73 draft nets, 4 drift nets, 1 bag net, 1 stake net, producing altogether a sum of £560 available for protection.

The fisheries of the Cork district have improved during the last six or seven years to a greater extent than any other in Ireland, and although, as the quantity of fish increases, the temptation to poachers is also greater, it is to be hoped that the exertions of the Conservators and proprietors of fisheries to improve these rivers, which have hitherto been so successful, will not be relaxed in the future. The same constant watchfulness which has of late years prevailed, will be necessary, if the improvement is to he maintained.

No. 4. Lismore District.

Extending from Ballycotton, in the County of Cork, to Helvick Head, in the County of Waterford.

As in many other districts, the capture of salmon in this was less in 1878 than in the previous year, in consequence of the exceptional weather which prevailed during a part of the fishing season.

The quantity of fish on the spawning beds has increased.

Offences against the Fishery Laws are reported to have diminished, although in consequence, it is presumed, of increased vigilance, the number of prosecutions was greater than in 1877.

Ninety-two persons were prosecuted for offences of various kinds against the Fishery Laws, of these 39 were at the instance of the Board of Conservators, and 53 by the Constabulary and Coast Guard, of the former 35 were convicted, and 4 were acquitted or dismissed, and of the latter 43 were convicted and 10 were acquitted or dismissed.

In my report for last year I referred to our proposed action, with a view of somewhat restricting the operation of the drift-net fishing which we were quite satisfied, as previously carried on, had injured the fisheries of the river. Accordingly the following Bye-Law was prepared by us, and, having been approved by Your Grace and Privy Council, is now in force.

"We, the Inspectors of Irish Fisheries, acting under the authority of the above-named Acts, do make and ordain this Bye-law, by which it is prohibited, and it is hereby prohibited, to use for the capture of salmon or trout any drift net in the tidal portion of the River Blackwater, or its tributaries, above or to the northward of a line drawn across said river from the townland boundary between the townlands of Strancally and Newport East on the west, to the townland boundary between the townlands of Coolbagh and Ballynaclash on the east, all in the County of Waterford. Any person offending against this Bye-law shall forfeit and pay for each offence a sum of Five Pounds, and all nets used contrary to this Bye-law shall be forfeited."

I am quite satisfied that this Bye-law will have a marked effect in increasing the productiveness of the district. Drift fishing in comparatively open water may, under certain restrictions be permitted, but on the narrow reaches of the river from which it will now be excluded, it was most injurious.

For Close season tables and Bye-laws in force, see pages 64 and 68 of the appendix.

In 1878 the following engines were licensed and used for taking salmon :—253 single rods, 6 cross lines, 25 snap nets, 11 draft nets, 106 drift nets, 1 pole net, 1 bag net, 2 stake weirs, 2 boxes or cribs, producing a sum of £745 10*s*. In addition to this £57 10*s*. 7*d*.

was received for fines, £5 10s. from the sale of forfeited engines, and £68 per-centage upon the Poor Law Valuation of Fisheries. The whole amounting to £876 10s. 7d. available for protection.

Although since 1868 the funds of the District have considerably increased, yet they are still totally insufficient to provide such protection as would secure the proper developement of the fisheries. This may easily be inferred by a reference to the Ordnance Survey Catchment Basin Map, which shows that the principal river, the Blackwater, has a length of 104 miles, with tributaries of 234, besides minor streams in which salmon deposit their ova, and two other rivers respectively 13¼ and 9 miles in length.

The present Clerk of the District, a most intelligent and energetic officer, recently gave us sworn evidence that the district was not properly watched, and that he considered it would require over £2,000 a year to secure proper protection, or nearly three times the sum available.

In this evidence, from my own experience, I fully concur.

At the conclusion of the Public Inquiry which we held in the Court House, Fermoy, on the 11th March last upon the drift net question, complaints were officially made to us as to the illegal condition of the Lismore Fishing Weir. In reply we intimated that the subject would be looked into, and that we would take such steps in regard to it as we might deem to be necessary.

Subsequently we made a full statement of the case to the authorities and requested sanction for the employment of a solicitor to enable us to bring the matter in proper legal form before the Magistrates at Petty Sessions, but the authority has not been granted.

The condition of this weir has long been a subject of complaint, and we have before now officially communicated with the agent of the proprietor, informing him that we considered that the "Free Gap in the Weir is not in conformity with the provisions of the Act 26 and 27 Vic., chapter 114."

For a considerable period the Conservators carried on legal proceedings to compel the owner to have the Gap placed in accordance with the law. They failed upon a point of law, and they will not now move further in the matter, as they consider the question should be taken up by this department.

There is no doubt that the funds of the district are insufficient to provide for legal expenses, and although it may be argued that individual proprietors should take up matters of this kind, none will come forward to do so, in order to settle a question which applies generally to all Ireland, and thus the provisions of the Act of 1863 become a dead letter.

Feeling that the question was a public one, and demanded our attention, we made the representation to which I have before referred.

No. 5—Waterford District.

Extending from Helvick Head, in the County of Waterford, to Kiln Bay (East of Bannon Bay), in the County of Wexford.

The condition of the Fisheries in 1878 I consider to have been as satisfactory as could be expected considering the peculiarities of the season.

In the early season the take of fish far exceeded the quantity taken in the corresponding period of 1877—say for the first three months:—the falling off from that period was very considerable, and can only be accounted for by the peculiarities of the season.

In my last report I referred to the dissatisfaction of the Conservators of the Upper Tidal Waters of the Rivers Nore and Barrow, who complained that the quantity of fish reaching the upper waters was decreasing, and that this decrease was caused by the increase of drift-nets on the lower Fisheries.

The inquiries held in 1877, and concluded in 1878, led to the following Bye-Law being prepared. I am very glad to my that having been since submitted to Your Grace and Privy Council, and having been approved, it is now in force:—

"We, the Inspectors of Irish Fisheries, acting under the authority of the above-named Acir, do make and ordain this Bye-Law, by which it is prohibited, and it is hereby prohibited, to use for the capture of Salmon or Trout any Drift Net in the Tidal portions of the River Suir, Nore, and Barrow, above a line drawn across said River from Checkpoint, County Waterford, on the west, in an easterly direction to Campile Pill, in the County of Wexford. Any person offending against this Bye-Law shall forfeit and pay for each offence a sum ot Five Pounds, and all Nets used contrary to this Bye-Law shall be forfeited."

The following extract from our report to the Privy Council, which accompanied the bye-law, will be interesting as showing the rapid increase of this description of engine fishing in the Waterford Estuary :—

2. "Before the Act of 1863, the number of drift nets used in these rivers in any year only amounted to 78; since then it has increased to 90, and in 1877 there were 77 of those nets used :—

"For the 13 years before the Act of 1863, up to the end of 1876, the average number of drift nets used was	20
For the 13 years since that Act the average number was	78
For the 7 years before the Act of 1863, the number was	26
For the 7 years after the Act of 1863, the number was	78
For the first 6 years during which there is any official record of the number used, viz., 1851 to 1856, the average number was	13

3. "Formerly, before the Act of 1863, these nets were used mainly seaward of the line proposed in our Bye-law, and never, except very occasionally, in the narrow parts of the rivers above this proposed line."

At the appeal which was argued before the Judicial Committee of the Privy Council against the bye-law, exhaustive evidence was taken with regard to it, and every argument was used to prevent its passing; but after mature deliberation, the Committee recommended that it should be sanctioned.

The rod fishings in the Suir are steadily increasing in value.

The average size of salmon is reported to have increased; they now average 14 lbs.

During 1878 there were 82 prosecutions for violations of the Fishery Laws before the magistrates at Petty Sessions, of these 79 resulted in convictions, and the offenders fined; the remaining three were acquitted.

For tables of Close seasons and the Bye-laws in force, see pp. 64 and 68 of Appendix.

The following engines for taking salmon were licensed and used in 1878;—216 salmon rods, 14 cross lines, 244 snap nets, 29 draft nets, 90 drift nets, 4 stake weirs, 3 boxes or cribs, and 22 gaps or eyes for eels. The amount received for License duty being £1,141. To this must be added £103 1*s.* 11*d.* received on account of fines, £3 9*s.* 4*d.* for the sale of forfeited engines, and £11 10*s.* 7*d.* interest on Bank deposits, making altogether a sum of £1,259 1*s.* 10*d.* available for protection, as compared with £1,173 11*s.* 4*d.* received for the previous year.

No. 2.—Wexford District.

Extending from Wicklow Head in the County of Wicklow to Kiln Bay (east of Bannow Bay), in the County of Wexford.

Although the fisheries in the district are reported to be "improving," yet the capture of salmon was less in 1878 than in 1877.

The number of fish on the spawning beds was greater than preceding year.

The size of the salmon taken is reported to be considerably larger than in previous years. The peale has not increased in size.

Offences against the Fishery Laws have decreased.

During the year 31 persons were summoned for offences against the Fishery Act; 29 of these prosecutions ended in convictions against the different persons; the remaining two were dismissed.

The close season tables and the bye-laws in force in this district will be seen at pages 64 and 68.

The following engines were licensed for fishing :—83 salmon rods, and 54 draft nets, producing, with £39 4*s.* 5*d.* received for fines, a sum of £284 4*s.* 5*d.*, available for protection as against £252 14*s.* 6*d.* received in 1877.

Concluding Observations.

The year of 1878 was not generally as productive as that of the previous year, but on the whole it may be considered about an average season.

The spring fishing commenced well, and gave promise of a most productive year, but as the season advanced the take of fish diminished, and the results not as satisfactory as were anticipated.

The rainfall for March and April in 1878 was much below that for 1877, viz. :—

	1877.	1878.
March, ...	2·576	1·159
April, ...	3·661	2·360

whilst in May and June this order was reversed, thus—

	1877.	1878.
May, ...	2·155	4·192
June, ...	1·087	5·389

In the earlier part of the season the nets in the lower fisheries were most effective, whilst later on the great quantity of water in the tidal parts of the rivers prevented their efficient working, but after all it is not easy to decide positively the cause of the diminished capture.

I have so often commented upon the fact, that in but few cases the amounts due to the district, upon the valuation of the different fisheries have been paid, that it appears almost useless again to draw attention to it. It is most important that this source of revenue should be closely looked after, and I must say, that I consider the avoidance of this very proper tax, reflects little credit upon owners of fisheries, who in many cases derive considerable incomes from them without any expenditure, beyond the payment of their ordinary license duty.

I have but little to add, further than to reiterate in the strongest manner my opinion, as expressed in former reports, of the necessity of revising the scale of license duties, and the result to be expected therefrom.

The Royal Irish Constabulary have rendered invaluable assistance in preservation during the close season, especially in the counties of Cork and Waterford, and I quite anticipate their good work will be shown by increased production in the future. The Coast Guard also have rendered good service in many ways.

Altogether I consider the fisheries of my division in a satisfactory condition.

JOS. HAYES.

MR. JOHNSTON'S REPORT.

Division extends from Wicklow Head to Mullaghmore, County Sligo, embracing in whole or part the Counties of Wicklow, Dublin, Kildare, King's County, Meath, Westmeath, Louth, Cavan, Longford, Monaghan, Down, Armagh, Antrim, Londonderry, Fermanagh, Tyrone, Donegal, Leitrim, and Sligo, and includes the eight Districts of Dublin, Drogheda, Dundalk, Ballycastle, Coleraine, Londonderry, Letterkenny, and Ballyshannon.

No. 1, or Dublin District

Extends from Wicklow Head to Skerries, county Dublin, embracing in part or whole the counties of Wicklow, Dublin, Kildare, and Meath.

Close Seasons.

Tidal Waters—From Howth to Dalkey Island—Between 15th August and 1st of February. For remainder of district—Between 15th September and 2nd March.

Fresh Water—Same. Angling with cross lines—Same. Angling with single rod and line—Between 31st October and 1st February.

Bye-Laws.—River Liffey.

Prohibiting the catching or attempting to catch salmon with any net of greater length than 350 yards between Island-bridge weir and a line drawn due north from Poolbeg Lighthouse.

Permitting the use of nets with meshes of one inch from knot to knot for the capture of salmon or trout between Dalkey Island and Wicklow Head.

Report.

The general state of the salmon fisheries in this district during 1878 has been prosperous.

There has, however, been a falling off in the number of engines used in this district as compared with 1877, in which year there were in use 109 salmon rods, 2 cross lines, and 14 draft nets. In 1878 the numbers were 97 salmon rods, 1 cross line, and 16 draft nets.

Consequently the receipts have fallen off. The amount taken for salmon rods being £97; for cross line, £2; and for draft nets, £48—making, with £4 4s. 10d. for fines—a total of £151 4s. 10d., as compared with £159 13s. 8d. in 1877.

The average weight of salmon taken was 10½ lbs.; that of peale 4 lbs.

The highest price given for salmon was 3s. 6d.; the lowest, 8d.; average, 1s. 6d. per lb.

The take of salmon and grilse in this district was about the same as in 1877, when it was fully double that of the preceding year.

There are no water bailiffs employed by the Board; but the Conservators allow the Swords Angling Club £10 per annum towards the protection of the Swords River. The Clerk of the Conservators acts as inspector of the district.

There are, however, six water bailiffs employed by private individuals—three by the Earl of Meath, one by Mr. R. Cane, of Celbridge, and two by the Swords Angling Club.

Great numbers of salmon have been destroyed in dry weather at the mouth of the Liffey, in consequence of the discharge of poisonous matter into the tideway of the river by the chemical works on the north and south quays.

There have been five successful prosecutions for breaches of the fishery laws during the year on the part of the Constabulary, with whom the Conservators co-operated, although not themselves prosecuting any persons. The value of the services of the Constabulary is, therefore, apparent, and it is hoped that they will still further endeavour to prevent the destruction of fry, which takes place on such portion of the rivers as are open to the public, where, under pretence of angling for trout, perch, and pike, the fry, in their descent to the sea, are killed in considerable numbers.

No. 17[1], or Drogheda District

Extends from Skerries, county Dublin, to Clogher Head, county Louth, and embraces portions of the counties of Dublin, Louth, King's County, Meath, Westmeath, and Cavan.

Close Seasons.

For all Engines—Between 4th August and 12th February.

No Bye-Laws.

Report.

The general state of the salmon fisheries in this district, in 1878, has been satisfactory. On the whole, there has been a considerable increase in the number of engines used in the district over 1877. There were, in 1878, in use—66 salmon rods, 5 cross lines, 6 snap nets, 61 draft nets, 5 boxes, and 44 eel nets.

The receipts have considerably increased since last year. They were, for salmon rods, £66; for cross lines, £10; for snap nets, £9; for draft nets, £183; for boxes, £50; and for eel nets £44; making, with £1 6s. 8d. for fines, a total of £363 6s. 8d., as compared with £322 17s. 1d. in 1877.

The average weight of salmon taken was 16 lbs.; of peale, 5 lbs.

The highest price given for salmon was 2s. 6d.; the lowest, 7d.; average, 1s. per lb.

Large captures of salmon were made in the spring, especially in tidal waters; but the summer fishing was below the average of former years. Grilse did not begin to run in any quantity till at and after the close of the season.

The stock of breeding fish continues to increase. The spawning beds have been every where fully occupied.

Fifteen water-bailiffs are employed by the Conservators, and one by Mr. J. L. W. Naper and others.

In one or two places there has been destruction of the fry, but that of spent fish has much diminished.

The number of persons prosecuted to conviction by the Conservators was eight; while sixteen were prosecuted to conviction by the Constabulary. The principal portion of the prosecutions in the former case was for fishing during the weekly close season; while the destruction of fish by flax-water flowing into rivers was watched over by the Constabulary.

No. 17[2], or Dundalk District

Extends from Clogher Head, county Louth, to Donaghadee, county Down, embracing, in whole or part, the counties of Louth, Meath, Down, Armagh, Monaghan, and Cavan.

Close Seasons.

For tidal and fresh waters, save in Annagassan, Glyde, Dee, Fane, and their tributaries—Between 31st August and 1st April. In Glyde, Dee, and Annagassan—Between 19th August and 12th February. Fane River—Between 19th August and 1st April.

Angling with cross lines—Same as netting. Angling with single rod—11th October to 1st of March, save in Annagassan, Glyde, and Dee. In Annagassan, Glyde, and Dee—Between 30th September and 1st of February.

Bye-Laws.

Prohibiting to catch, or attempting to catch, salmon or trout with any net of greater length than 500 yards between Clogher Head and Ballagan Point, county Louth.

Prohibiting the catching, or attempting to catch, salmon in any tidal water between Dunany Point and Soldiers' Point, county Louth, with a spear, lyster, otter, strokehaul, dree-draw, or gaff, except when the latter is used as an auxiliary with rod and line, or for removing fish from any legal weir or box by the owner or occupier thereof.

Report.

The general state of the salmon fisheries in this district during 1878 was satisfactory, a continued improvement having taken place.

There has been an increase in the number of engines used in the district as compared with 1877; the number in 1878 being 47 salmon rods (two more than in any other year since the district was formed), 25 draft nets, 2 bag nets, 1 head weir, and 35 eel nets.

The receipts have also very largely increased this year. They were, for salmon rods, £47; for draft nets, £75; for bag nets, £20; for a head weir, £6; for eel nets, £35.

The amount received from fines was £42 15*s.* 6*d.*; rates on Poor Law valuation of several fisheries, £8; subscription received, £5 10*s.* The total receipts amounted to £239 5*s.* 6*d.*, as compared with £187 10*s.* 8*d.* in 1877.

The average weight of the salmon taken was 15 lbs.; that of peale 8 lbs. This shows a considerable increase over 1877.

The take of salmon and grilse in the district was more productive than in 1877, which is attributable to the high floods in May and June.

The highest price given for salmon was 2*s.* per lb.; the lowest, 1*s.*; average, 1*s.* 6*d.* per lb.

The quantity of breeding fish observed in the rivers was much greater than in 1877, in which year it was considerably over that of 1876.

Twenty-six water bailiffs are employed by the Conservators, for various periods of time, from one to four months, in one case for the whole year. There is, also, an Inspector of Water-Bailiffs employed for ten months.

Twenty-six prosecutions were instituted by the Conservators. In eight of these the cases were dismissed, while four were reversed on appeal.

Thirty prosecutions were instituted by the Constabulary, whose activity and energy in this district, in enforcing the fishery laws, deserve praise.

There is a great deal of unlicensed fishing in certain parts of the district, notwithstanding the vigilance of the Clerk to the Conservators and of the Constabulary. The Board have taken all possible care of the district; but certain small rivers, at a distance from Dundalk, have hitherto been to them a source of considerable loss. It is designed to attempt to remedy this state of things by forming a new district.

No. 16[1], or Ballycastle District

Extends from Donaghadee, county Down, to Portrush, county Antrim, containing portions of the counties of Down, Antrim, and Derry.

Close Seasons.

Tidal—Between 19th August and 4th February.

Fresh Water—19th August and 1st March. Cross lines—28th September and 16th March. Single rod and line—1st November and 1st February.

Engines used in 1877—25 salmon rods, 12 draft nets, and 14 bag nets.

Bye-Laws—Bush River.

Repealing definition of Bush River Estuary, as fixed by late Special Commissioners on 8th February, 1864.

Report.

The general state of the salmon fisheries, in this district, during 1878, was not satisfactory. There has been a slight falling off in the number of engines used in the district, compared with 1877. There were in use, in 1878, 32 salmon rods, 11 draft nets, and 14 bag nets.

The receipts were, for salmon rods, £22; for draft nets, £33; for bag nets, £140; making, with £32 11*s.* 3*d.* fines, and £60, rates on Poor Law valuation of several fisheries, a total of £287 11*s.* 3*d.*, as compared with £281 5*s.*, in 1877. From the apparent total receipts, £3 must be deducted; as, in one case, a draft net licence was irregularly issued without payment.

The average weight of salmon taken was about 7 lbs. The highest price given was 1*s.* 10*d.*; the lowest 8*d.*; average 10*d.* per lb. The take of salmon was less productive than in 1877.

The quantity of breeding fish observed was, also, less than in 1877.

No bailiffs are employed by the Board; but each proprietor of a fishery receives a certain sum, to be devoted to the payment of the bailiffs in his employ. For these payments certified vouchers have been produced, and entered in the accounts of the Board.

About thirty-five bailiffs are employed by private individuals—Sir F. E. Macnaghten, bart., Sir Frederick Boyd, bart., the Earl of Antrim, and Mr. John Finlay.

The neighbourhood of Stranocum, on the Bush, continues to be pre-eminent for poaching. Outrages, time after time, have been committed there, during the breeding season; and scenes of violence and lawlessness, constantly occurring, are calculated to demoralize the neighbourhood. An adequate force of police, for the protection of the water-bailiffs and the preservation of the peace of the locality, at any rate during the months of November, December, and January, is indispensable; and it is to be regretted that, though Sir Francis E. Macnaghten has offered to provide a house, and pay all expenses, if such a force was provided, he has been unable to obtain the men. If such an arrangement be not made, the Conservators consider that it will be necessary to place fire-arms in the hands of the water-bailiffs, for the protection of their lives, when in the discharge of their duty.

No. 15[a], or Coleraine District

Extends from Portrush, county Antrim, to Downhill boundary, county Derry, embracing parts of the counties Monaghan, Armagh, Down, Antrim, and Derry.

Close Seasons.

Tidal portion—Between 19th August and 4th February.

Fresh Water—Between 19th August and 1st March. Angling with single rods—Between 19th October and 16th March, save Bann and its tributaries. For Bann and its tributaries—Between 31st October and 1st March. Cross lines—28th September and 16th March. Pollen fishing by trammel nets in Lough Neagh—Between 31st October and 1st February.

Bye-Laws—Lough Neagh.

Prohibiting the use of draft nets for the capture of pollen.

Permitting pollen to be taken by trammel or set nets, composed of yarn of a fine texture, not less than ten hanks to the pound weight, doubled and twisted with a mesh of not less than one inch from knot to knot, between 1st February and 31st October.

Prohibiting the snatching or attempting to snatch salmon in any of the tidal or fresh waters of district.

Report.

The general state of the salmon fisheries, in this district, during 1878, was not quite so good as the previous year.

There was an increase in the total number of engines used in the district, over 1877, principally in trammel nets. There were in use, in 1878, 91 salmon rods, 135 draft nets, 108 trammel nets (as against 88, in 1877), 2 bag nets, 4 boxes, and 52 eel nets.

The receipts for 1878 were, for salmon rods, £91; draft nets, £405; trammel nets, £108; bag nets, £20; boxes, cribs, &c., £40; eel nets, £156; fines, £149 6*s.* 9*d.*; rates on Poor Law valuation of several fisheries, £210—making a total of £1,179 6*s.* 9*d.*, as compared with £1,105 8*s.* 2*d.* in 1877.

The average weight of salmon taken was about 10 lbs. The highest price given for salmon was 2*s.*; the lowest 10*d.*;—average 1*s.* per lb. The take of salmon and grilse, in the lower or tidal portion of the district, was about equal to that of 1877; but, in the upper or freshwater portion, it was much less productive, owing to the dryness of the season.

The quantity of breeding fish observed was much less than in the previous year; when it exceeded that of 1876.

Sixty-three water-bailiffs and three inspectors are employed for the whole year by the Conservators; and three water-bailiffs by Mr. S. M. Alexander, and Mr. E. J. Harland.

The number of prosecutions by the Conservators was one hundred and thirty-two, of which fifty-two were for flax-water pollution; those undertaken by the constabulary amounted to thirty-three.

There was one very serious case, in which an inspector of water-bailiffs, and two of his men, after seizing a large number of nets, on Lough Neagh, were attacked by two boats full of men, and severely beaten, and the nets rescued. For this six men were prosecuted, convicted, and fined. The punishment seems inadequate to the offence.

It is desirable that the Constabulary should be instructed to render assistance, when necessary, without the loss of time consequent upon swearing informations; as, very often, during the delay, offenders against the fishery laws make their escape.

Inquiries were held at Toomebridge, on the 9th October, and at Coleraine, on the 10th October, by the Inspectors, and it was decided to make a Bye-Law prohibiting any boat, cot, or curragh, in the district, having on board thereof any net for the capture of salmon or trout in the tidal waters during the weekly close season, between the hours of 12 noon, on Saturday, and 4 A.M., on Monday. And also prohibiting any net for the capture of salmon, trout, or pollen, being on board in Lough Neagh or Lough Beg, between 11 A.M., on Saturday, and 4 A.M., on Monday morning. In consequence of large quantities of fish having been sent away by rail, during the annual close season, it is desirable that the authorities should have power to examine boxes and parcels supposed to contain salmon, trout, or pollen, during that season.

No. 15[1], or Londonderry District

Extends from Downhill boundary, county Derry, to Malin Head, county Donegal includes parts of Derry, Donegal, and Tyrone.

Close Seasons.

Tidal—Between 31st August and 15th April.

Fresh Water—Same. Angling with cross lines—28th September and 15th April Angling with single rod—Between 1st November and 1st February.

Bye-Laws.

Permitting the use of nets for capture of fish other than salmon and trout with meshes of half an inch from knot to knot in Baronscourt Lakes and Streams.

Permitting the use of nets with meshes of one inch from knot to knot in Lough Foyle and tidal parts of the river.

Prohibiting having nets for the capture of salmon or trout in or on board any boat, cot, or curragh, in the tidal waters of said district, which comprises the whole of the sea along the coast between Malin Head, in the county of Donegal, and the townland boundary between the townlands of Drumagully and Downhill, in the county of Londonderry, with the whole of the tideway along said coast and rivers and the whole of the tidal portion of the several rivers and their tributaries flowing into said coast between said points, at any time *between the hours of Twelve of the Clock at noon on Saturday, and Four of the Clock on Monday Morning.*

Report.

The general state of the salmon fisheries in this district was fairly good.

There has been an increase in the number of salmon rods, cross lines, and drift nets used, and a slight decrease in the other engines for taking fish. The number in use in 1878 was—77 salmon rods, 6 cross lines, 32 draft nets, 44 drift nets, 2 pole nets, 4 bag nets, and 3 stake nets.

The receipts were, for salmon rods, £77; cross lines, £12; draft nets, £96; drift nets, £132; pole nets, £4; bag nets, £40; stake nets, 90; with £46 18*s.* 3*d.* for fines; amount of rates on Poor Law Valuation on several fisheries, £95; subscriptions from lessees of the Irish Society, £605; making a total of £1,197 18*s.* 3*d.*, as against £699 4*s.* 2*d.* in 1877.

The average weight of salmon taken was 11 lbs.; of peale, 6½ lbs. The highest price given for salmon was 1s. 6*d.*; the lowest, 8*d.*; average, 10*d.* per lb.

The take of salmon and grilse in the district was less than in 1877.

The quantity of breeding fish observed was less than in 1877.

There was a considerable destruction of fry, during their descent to the sea, by unlicensed anglers, who say they fish for brown trout.

About 190 Water Bailiffs are employed by the Conservators from October to March, and a few during the entire year. The lessees of tho Irish Society employ about 40 Bailiffs.

In consequence of complaints made to the Inspectors in regard to breaches of the weekly close season, we held inquiries at Londonderry, on the 24th April, and Moville on the 26th. From the evidence then given it was deemed expedient to enact a Bye-Law, prohibiting the practice of keeping any net for the capture of salmon or trout, in or on board any boat, cot, or curragh, in the tidal waters of this district, between 12 o'clock, noon, on Saturdays, and 4 o'clock on Monday mornings.

This Bye-Law has been approved by the Lord Lieutenant and Privy Council of Ireland.

A Bye-Law which awaits similar approval has also been made, prohibiting anyone to have in possession, between sunrise and sunset, at any season of the year, on or near the upper or fresh water portions of the rivers in this district, any spear, lyster, stroke-haul, or gaff, except when the latter may be used solely as auxiliary to angling for salmon legally, with rod and line.

The former Bye-Law remedies a practice noticed in the report for 1877, of my predecessor, Mr. Blake, whose lengthened and varied experience in connexion with Irish Fisheries rendered any suggestion of his especially valuable.

No. 14, or Letterkenny District

Extends from Malin Head to Rossan Point, county Donegal, and comprises the greater part of the county Donegal.

Close Seasons.

Tidal Water—Between 19th August and 4th February, and one mile above tideway, save Crana or Buncrana and Gweebarra Rivers. For Crana or Buncrana—Between 14th September and 15th April. For Gweebarra—Between 30th September and 1st April.

Fresh Water—Between 19th August and 1st March, save Crana or Buncrana River, Leenane and Gweebarra rivers, which are the same as tidal. Angling with cross lines—Same as netting in fresh water. Angling with single rod and line—Between 1st November and 1st February; save in Buncrana. Crana or Buncrana—Between 31st October and 1st March.

Bye-Law.

Permitting the use of nets for the capture of salmon or trout, with meshes of one inch from knot to knot, in the Crana or Buncrana river, and within one mile seawards and coastwards thereof.

Report.

The general state of the salmon fisheries, in this district, is good.

Except in the number of salmon rods, of which there were 7 less in 1878 than in 1877, there was, for the most part, a considerable increase in the engines used, over the previous year. In 1878, there were 46 salmon rods, 16 draft nets, 13 drift nets, 3 bag nets, 1 box, and 6 loop nets.

The receipts were, for salmon rods, £46; draft nets, £48; drift nets, £39; bag nets, £30; box, £10; loop nets, £6. The fines amounted to £3 15*s.* 5*d.*; sale of forfeited engines, 3*s.*; rates on Poor Law valuation of several fisheries, £14. The total amount of the annual receipts was £196 18*s.* 5*d.* (not including £1 16*s.* 5*d.*, interest on balance in Bank) as against £189 6*s.* 8*d.* received in 1877.

The average weight of salmon taken was 9¼ lbs.; of peale, 6 lbs. The highest price given was 2*s.*, the lowest 4*d.*—average 8*d.* per lb.

The take of salmon and grilse in the district was less than in 1877.

The quantity of breeding fish observed is reported to be, also, much less.

One hundred and twenty-three are employed. Of these, 105 are employed for the whole year, and 18 during the close season, on the properties of the Marquis of

Conyngham, Lord Cloncurry, Lord George Hill, Sir James Stewart, and Messrs. Stewart, Olpherts, and Richardson.

The number of prosecutions instituted by the Conservators, in 1878, was 11, out of which there were 6 convictions. There were 8 persons prosecuted by the Constabulary, all of whom, except 2 were convicted.

The number of offences against the fishery laws have decreased.

It is satisfactory to be able to state that the Board has obtained the services of an efficient clerk, who will act as an inspector, in the district. The accounts for the year have been carefully kept, and there appears a balance in Bank of £270 3s. 5d.

No. 13, or Ballyshannon District

Extends from Rossan Point, county Donegal, to Mullaghmore, county Sligo.

Close Seasons.

For tidal and fresh waters—Between 19th August and 1st March, save River Eske and tributaries, which is 17th September and 1st April.

For angling with single rods—Between 9th October and 1st March, save Bunduff, which is between 30th September and 1st February; Bundrowes, between 30th September and 1st January, and, save Erne, between 30th September and 1st March.

Bye-Laws.

Permitting use of nets with meshes of one inch from knot to knot in tideway of River Erne.

Repealing bye-law of 24th February, 1860, prohibiting use of nets with meshes less than one inch for capture of fish of any kind on that part of the coast of the county Donegal inside or to the north-east and north of lines drawn from Rossan Point to Teelin Head, and from Teelin Head to Carrigan Head, and from Carrigan Head to Muckross Point, all in the barony of Bannagh and county of Donegal.

Permitting use of nets with meshes of one inch from knot to knot, for capture of fish by persons having right to use nets in Lough Erne, between Enniskillen and Belleek, between 1st May and first day of close season in each year.

Prohibiting the capture of fish of any description with the instrument commonly called and known by the name of the Spoonbait, or any other instrument of the like nature or device, during the months of January, February, and March in each year, in that part of the River Erne situated between the Falls of Belleek and a line drawn due south across the river, from the point of Castlecaldwell demesne, by the eastern point of the Muckinish, or White Island, to the opposite bank, all in the county of Fermanagh.

Permitting use of nets for the capture of fish with meshes of one inch from knot to knot (to be measured along the side of the square, or four inches to be measured all round each such mesh, such measurements being taken in the clear when the net is wet), within so much of the River Eany Water, or Inver, in the county of Donegal, as lies above the mouth of said river as defined.

Report.

The general state of the salmon fisheries in this district, during 1878, was good; though the take of salmon and grilse was less productive than in 1877.

The receipts for 1878 were, for salmon rods, £112; cross line and rods, £26; draft nets, £135; pole nets, £6; stake weirs, £30; box, &c., £40; eel nets, £29; from fines, £12 15s. 6d.; rates on Poor-law valuation of several fisheries, £5; interest on bank account £7 1s. 2d.; subscriptions received, £168 2s.; total, £570 18s. 8d., as against £401 10s. in 1877.

The engines used were 112 salmon rods, 13 cross lines, 45 draft nets, 3 pole nets, 1 stake net, 4 boxes or cribs, and 29 gaps or eyes for eels.

The average weight of salmon taken was, 11½ lbs.; of peale, 7 lbs. The highest price given for salmon was 2s. 4d.; the lowest 10d.; the average price was 1s. per lb. Less breeding fish were observed in the district than in 1877.

Six prosecutions by the Conservators are reported. In 1877, the number was twelve. Two hundred bailiffs are employed by the Conservators, and three by the Marquis of Ely. Offences against the fishery laws are reported as on the increase.

Concluding Remarks.

Having only had the honour of acting as one of the Inspectors of Irish Fisheries during a portion of 1878, I shall not presume, this year, to offer many observations.

The Inspectors after inquiry held in Downpatrick, on 7th October, and having received requisitions unanimously agreed to by the Boards of Conservators of the Dundalk and Ballycastle districts, have decided to form a new district, extending from Ballagan Point, county Louth, to Carrickfergus, county Antrim, to be called Down district, bearing the number 16². This step has been taken in order that the fisheries of that portion of Dundalk district lying in the county Down might receive more attention, and be further, it is hoped, developed, in the Quoile, and other rivers.

Matters which seem to call for the interference of the Executive or the Legislature more properly belong to the General Report.

WM. JOHNSTON.

In forwarding our individual reports upon the Salmon Fisheries in the divisions under our respective supervision, we consider it necessary to inform Your Grace that in regard to the observation respecting the Lismore and Listowel Weirs, and the removal of Fixed Engines in the River Shannon from the situations shewn in the several certificates, we are all of the opinion expressed by the Inspectors of the Districts.

The subjects referred to have, from time to time, received our most careful and anxious consideration, and we consider, if steps are not taken to enforce compliance with the provisions of the Act of 1863 and 1869, the result may, in the end, be very detrimental to the fisheries.

There are a few matters which require amendment by legislation, and on which we shall be prepared, if called upon, to submit our views to the Government.

As we have in the different reports gone fully into all details which we consider of importance, both as regards the Sea and Inland Fisheries, we beg to submit them for Your Grace's information without further comment.

We have the honour to be,

Your Grace's very obedient servants,

THOS. F. BRADY.
JOS. HAYES.
WM. JOHNSTON.

Alan Hornsby, *Secretary.*

Office of Irish Fisheries,
31st *March*, 1879.

APPENDIX.

No. 1.—List of Defaulters in Repayments under Irish Reproductive Loan Fund Act, and Loans Recalled.

Defaulters in Repayment of Instalments.

County.	Year.	Application Number.	Names.	Instalment. £	s.	d.	Date due.
Mayo, . .	1875,	50	Dominick and James Moran, .	0	17	6	1st August, 1878.
Do. . .	"	51	Michael Moran, . . .	0	17	6	1st August, 1878.
				0	17	6	1st September, 1878.
Do. . .	"	79	James Kennedy, . . .	2	13	2	1st October, 1878.
Do. . .	"	109	Dominick Grehan, . . .	1	15	0	1st August, 1878.
Do. . .	"	132	Michael Lavelle, Michael Caulfield, Thomas Davis, . . .	2	2	0	1st February, 1878.
				2	2	0	1st August, 1878.
Do. . .	"	133	Hugh and Patrick Monaghan, and Francis Tougher, . . .	0	14	0	1st August, 1876.
				2	2	0	1st February, 1877.
				2	2	0	1st August, 1877.
				2	2	0	1st February, 1878.
				2	2	0	1st August, 1878.
Do. . .	"	237	Pat Loftus and Pat Sullivan, .	1	15	0	1st August, 1877.
				1	15	0	1st August, 1878.
Do. . .	1876,	15	John O'Malley and James Murphy,	2	2	0	1st April, 1877.
				2	2	0	1st October, 1877.
				2	2	0	1st April, 1878.
				2	2	0	1st October, 1878.
Do. . .	"	81	John Sullivan, . . .	2	2	0	1st January, 1878.
				2	2	0	1st July, 1878.
Do. . .	"	130	Michael and Thomas Doherty, and John Reilly, . . .	1	15	0	Do.
Do. . .	"	228	Martin Harte, . . .	1	11	1	Do.
Do. . .	"	275	Thomas Reilly, . . .	1	11	2	1st January, 1878.
				1	11	2	1st July, 1878.
Do. . .	"	285	David Reilly, . . .	0	8	0	1st July, 1877.
				1	8	0	1st January, 1878.
				1	8	0	1st July, 1878.
Do. . .	1877,	112	Thomas Barrett, . . .	1	17	3	1st August, 1878.
Do. . .	"	217	William Bournes, jun., . .	2	5	1	Do.
Clare, . .	1875,	17	M. Daly, ...	0	17	6	1st February, 1878.
Do. . .	"	32	M. Conolan, ...	0	13	4	Do.
Do. . .	"	93	J. and F. Hennessy, . . .	1	1	0	1st March, 1878.
				1	1	0	1st August, 1878.
				1	1	0	1st September, 1878.
Do. . .	"	144	J. Callaghan, . . .	0	17	6	1st February, 1878.
Do. . .	1876,	364	Francis and M. Keane, . .	2	2	0	1st December, 1878.
Do. . .	1877,	10	John Fennell, . . .	1	11	11	1st March, 1878.
Do. . .	"	27	John Crotty (John), and Martin Finnell, . . .	2	2	0	1st June, 1878.
				2	2	0	1st December, 1878.
Do. . .	"	341	Peter Shannon, . . .	1	15	0	1st September, 1878.
Do. . .	"	42	James Donoghue, . . .	1	1	0	1st December, 1878.
Sligo, . .	1875,	1,130	M. Leyden, ...	2	12	6	1st March, 1878.
				2	12	6	1st September, 1878.
Do. . .	"	1,330	J. Carway, ...	2	1	6	1st December, 1877.
				2	1	6	1st June, 1878.
Do. . .	1876,	52	John Costelloe, . . .	1	6	7	1st November, 1878.
Do. . .	1877,	404	A. Burke, ...	2	2	0	1st September, 1878.
Do. . .	"	433	P. Cavanagh, . . .	3	3	0	Do.
Galway, .	1875,	720	Michael Holleran, sen., and John M'Donnell, . . .	2	12	6	1st February, 1878.
				2	12	6	1st August, 1878.
Do. . .	1876,	19	J. M'Donough, jun., . . .	2	2	0	1st December, 1878.
Do. . .	"	89	M. Holleran, sen., . . .	2	12	6	Do.
Do. . .	"	100	Thomas Cooke, . . .	1	15	0	Do.
Do. . .	"	101	Stephen Toole, Michael Lacey (Wm.), Michael Cloonan, Patrick Adley, . . .	3	10	0	Do.
Do. . .	"	146	P. Lacey and P. Mongan, . .	2	12	6	Do.
Do. . .	"	147	P. and M. Davis, . . .	2	12	6	Do.
Do. . .	"	192	B. Burke, ...	1	15	0	Do.
Do. . .	1878,	127	P. Mulavil, ...	1	0	9	Do.

APPENDIX I.—DEFAULTERS in Repayments—*continued.*

County.	Year.	Application Number.	Names.	Instalment. £ s. d.	Date due.
CORK,	1875,	578	R. Maguire,	3 10 0 3 10 0	1st March, 1878. 1st September, 1878.
Do.	„	646	A. Harrington,	2 12 6 2 12 6	1st February, 1878. 1st August, 1878.
Do.	„	847	Cornelius M'Carthy,	2 12 6	1st September, 1878.
Do.	1876,	9	Denis O'Leary,	8 15 0	1st December, 1878.
Do.	„	62	P. Donovan,	2 12 6	1st November, 1878.
Do.	„	175	Bartholomew Walsh,	2 12 6	1st June, 1878.
Do.	„	266	William Skinner,	3 10 0	1st December, 1878.
Do.	„	267	Florence O'Leary,	4 7 6	Do.
KERRY,	1875,	180	T. and J. Foley,	3 6 6 3 6 6	1st March, 1878. 1st September, 1878.
Do.	„	290	J. Shea, jun.,	1 15 0	Do.
Do.	„	822	M. O'Connor,	5 5 0 5 5 0 5 5 0	1st September, 1877. 1st March, 1878. 1st September, 1878.
Do.	„	1,187	M. Fitzpatrick,	3 10 0	Do.
Do.	„	1,334	T. O'Connor,	3 19 10 3 19 10 3 19 10	1st October, 1877. 1st April, 1878. 1st October, 1878.
Do.	1876,	185	P. Keating,	4 7 6	1st December, 1878.
Do.	„	349	J. Segerson,	3 10 0	1st November, 1878.
Do.	1877,	288	J. Brennan,	3 10 0	1st December, 1878.
Do.	„	446	Timothy Foley,	5 1 6	1st August, 1878.

LOANS RECALLED TO 31ST DECEMBER, 1878.

County.	Year.	Application No.	Name of Borrower.	Address.	Amount of Loan Advanced. £ s. d.	Date Recalled.	Date Repaid.
MAYO,	1877	430	Patrick Browne, jun.,	Money, Westport,	12 0 0	27 Sept. 1878	
CLARE,	„	3	Denis Quinlan,	Carrigaholt,	6 0 0	30 Mar. 1878	
Do.	„	4	Thomas Knight,	Newtown, Carrigaholt,	12 0 0	22 Nov. 1877	
Do.	„	11	John Hickey,	Ross, do.	20 0 0	Do.	
Do.	„	13	Pat Glear and Michael Howe,	Lisnamoy,	12 0 0	13 Nov. 1877	17 Dec. 1877
Do.	„	20	Thomas Brumfill,	Kilcloher, Carrigaholt,	12 0 0	17 Nov. 1877	
Do.	„	27	Edmund Fennell,	Ross, do.	10 0 0	15 Dec. 1877	
Do.	„	94	Michael Scanlon, John M'Mahon,	Newtown, do. Moveen, do.	10 0 0	22 Nov. 1877	
Do.	„	97	Stephen Collins (Peter), Thos. Collins, and James Keane,	Tullig, do. Rahona, do.	12 0 0	8 June, 1878	
Do.	„	428	Denis Crowe,	Kilcredaun, do.	6 0 0	12 Apr. 1878	
SLIGO,	1875	582	Luke Feeny,	Ballyconnell, Ballinafull,	15 0 0	29 Mar. 1876	
Do.	1875	118	James Moffatt,	Strandhill, Sligo,	20 0 0	18 Dec. 1876	5 June, 1877
Do.	1878	266	Terence Leyden, jun.,	Upper Rosses, Rosses Point,	24 0 0	13 Dec. 1878	
GALWAY,	1877	208	Michael Coyne and Thomas Joyce,	Mullaghglass, Letterfrack,	10 0 0	11 Oct. 1878	31 Jan. 1879
Do.	„	209	Patrick and John Malley, Thomas Conneely, and John Malley,	Gortacnagiegh, do. Dawros, do. Mullaghglass, do.	15 0 0	6 June, 1878	27 Feb. 1879
Do.	„	210	Gregory Conneely, John do. (Patrick) Peter do. John do. (Gregory)	Gortacnagiegh, do.	20 0 0	12 Apr. 1878	1 June, 1878
Do.	„	211	Patrick and Michael Murray, John Keane and John M'Donnell,	Ardnagreevagh, do.	20 0 0	6 June, 1878	28 Jan. 1879
Do.	„	223	William, John, and Patrick Hearne,	Gortacnagiegh, do.	10 0 0	Do.	8 Aug. 1878
Do.	„	229	Joseph Conneely, Michael Mulkerrin, Thomas Hearne and Joseph J. Conneely,	Do. do.	16 0 0	Do.	6 Aug. 1878
Do.	„	264	Martin Coyne,	Bunnoga, do.	15 0 0	14 June, 1878	3 Oct. 1878 20 Jan. 1879
Do.	„	379	Richard King,	Cloon, Cleggan, do.	10 0 0	Do.	27 Aug. 1878
Do.	„	409	Darby Hearne,	Lettergesh, Letterfrack,	10 0 0	6 June, 1878	20 Jan. 1879
Do.	„	410	John Hynes,	[illegible], Renvyle,	10 0 0	5 Feb. 1878	21 Feb. 1878
Do.	„	411	Michael King,	Lettergesh, Letterfrack,	10 0 0	6 June, 1878	
Do.	„	412	Thomas Oorery,	Do. do.	10 0 0	Do.	31 Jan. 1879
CORK,	1875	263	R. Minahane,	Ballyrally, Skibbereen,	25 0 0	13 Dec. 1875	26 Jan. 1876
Do.	„	850	Patrick Keohane,	Toehead, Castletownsend,	20 0 0	4 Jan. 1876	3 Mar. 1876
Do.	1876	43	Daniel Collins,	Downeen, Rosscarbery,	10 0 0	9 July, 1878	29 July, 1878
Do.	1877	483	Thomas D. Notter,	Crookhaven, Skibbereen,	100 0 0	24 Oct. 1878	1 Nov. 1878
Do.	„	487	John Regan and John Hurley,	Ballinlough, [illegible],	15 0 0	7 Aug. 1878	
Do.	1878	34	John Sweeney,	[illegible], do.	35 0 0	4 July, 1878	
KERRY,	1875	181	Thomas Lynch,	Ballinamanig, Dingle,	30 0 0	24 Feb. 1876	26 Apr. 1876
Do.	1876	16	Michael Sullivan,	Farranreagh, Valentia,	100 0 0	18 Nov. 1878	
Do.	„	117	Michael and Timothy Sullivan,	Boolakeel, Cahirciveen,	35 0 0	8 Nov. 1878	30 Jan. 1879
Do.	1878	287	Patrick Shea,	Ballinskelligs,	12 0 0	Do.	11 Mar. 1879
Do.	„	486	James Moran,	Meelagulleen, Cahirciveen,	20 0 0	16 Dec. 1878	

APPENDIX No. 2.—ABSTRACT of RETURNS from COAST-GUARD of the NUMBERS of VESSELS, BOATS, and CREWS, engaged in the SEA FISHERIES in 1871.

No.	Name of District	Registering Officer	Solely engaged in Fishing									Only partially employed in Fishing									Totals			No.
			First Class			Second Class			Third Class			First Class			Second Class			Third Class						
			Vessels	Men	Boys	Vessels	Men	Boys	Vessels	Men	Boys	Vessels	Men	Boys	Vessels	Men	Boys	Vessels	Men	Boys	Vessels	Men	Boys	
[illegible]	Dublin	[illegible]	[illegible]	[illegible]	[illegible]	[illegible]	[illegible]	[illegible]	[illegible]	[illegible]	[illegible]	[illegible]	[illegible]	[illegible]	[illegible]	[illegible]	[illegible]	[illegible]	[illegible]	[illegible]	[illegible]	[illegible]	[illegible]	[illegible]
[illegible]	Arklow	[illegible]	[illegible]	[illegible]	[illegible]	[illegible]	[illegible]	[illegible]	[illegible]	[illegible]	[illegible]	[illegible]	[illegible]	[illegible]	[illegible]	[illegible]	[illegible]	[illegible]	[illegible]	[illegible]	[illegible]	[illegible]	[illegible]	[illegible]
[illegible]	Wexford	[illegible]	[illegible]	[illegible]	[illegible]	[illegible]	[illegible]	[illegible]	[illegible]	[illegible]	[illegible]	[illegible]	[illegible]	[illegible]	[illegible]	[illegible]	[illegible]	[illegible]	[illegible]	[illegible]	[illegible]	[illegible]	[illegible]	[illegible]
[illegible]	Waterford	[illegible]	[illegible]	[illegible]	[illegible]	[illegible]	[illegible]	[illegible]	[illegible]	[illegible]	[illegible]	[illegible]	[illegible]	[illegible]	[illegible]	[illegible]	[illegible]	[illegible]	[illegible]	[illegible]	[illegible]	[illegible]	[illegible]	[illegible]
[illegible]	Youghal	[illegible]	[illegible]	[illegible]	[illegible]	[illegible]	[illegible]	[illegible]	[illegible]	[illegible]	[illegible]	[illegible]	[illegible]	[illegible]	[illegible]	[illegible]	[illegible]	[illegible]	[illegible]	[illegible]	[illegible]	[illegible]	[illegible]	[illegible]
[illegible]	Queenstown	[illegible]	[illegible]	[illegible]	[illegible]	[illegible]	[illegible]	[illegible]	[illegible]	[illegible]	[illegible]	[illegible]	[illegible]	[illegible]	[illegible]	[illegible]	[illegible]	[illegible]	[illegible]	[illegible]	[illegible]	[illegible]	[illegible]	[illegible]
[illegible]	Kinsale	[illegible]	[illegible]	[illegible]	[illegible]	[illegible]	[illegible]	[illegible]	[illegible]	[illegible]	[illegible]	[illegible]	[illegible]	[illegible]	[illegible]	[illegible]	[illegible]	[illegible]	[illegible]	[illegible]	[illegible]	[illegible]	[illegible]	[illegible]
[illegible]	Skibbereen	[illegible]	[illegible]	[illegible]	[illegible]	[illegible]	[illegible]	[illegible]	[illegible]	[illegible]	[illegible]	[illegible]	[illegible]	[illegible]	[illegible]	[illegible]	[illegible]	[illegible]	[illegible]	[illegible]	[illegible]	[illegible]	[illegible]	[illegible]
[illegible]	Castletown Berehaven	[illegible]	[illegible]	[illegible]	[illegible]	[illegible]	[illegible]	[illegible]	[illegible]	[illegible]	[illegible]	[illegible]	[illegible]	[illegible]	[illegible]	[illegible]	[illegible]	[illegible]	[illegible]	[illegible]	[illegible]	[illegible]	[illegible]	[illegible]
[illegible]	[illegible]	[illegible]	[illegible]	[illegible]	[illegible]	[illegible]	[illegible]	[illegible]	[illegible]	[illegible]	[illegible]	[illegible]	[illegible]	[illegible]	[illegible]	[illegible]	[illegible]	[illegible]	[illegible]	[illegible]	[illegible]	[illegible]	[illegible]	[illegible]
[illegible]	[illegible]	[illegible]	[illegible]	[illegible]	[illegible]	[illegible]	[illegible]	[illegible]	[illegible]	[illegible]	[illegible]	[illegible]	[illegible]	[illegible]	[illegible]	[illegible]	[illegible]	[illegible]	[illegible]	[illegible]	[illegible]	[illegible]	[illegible]	[illegible]
[illegible]	[illegible]	[illegible]	[illegible]	[illegible]	[illegible]	[illegible]	[illegible]	[illegible]	[illegible]	[illegible]	[illegible]	[illegible]	[illegible]	[illegible]	[illegible]	[illegible]	[illegible]	[illegible]	[illegible]	[illegible]	[illegible]	[illegible]	[illegible]	[illegible]
[illegible]	[illegible]	[illegible]	[illegible]	[illegible]	[illegible]	[illegible]	[illegible]	[illegible]	[illegible]	[illegible]	[illegible]	[illegible]	[illegible]	[illegible]	[illegible]	[illegible]	[illegible]	[illegible]	[illegible]	[illegible]	[illegible]	[illegible]	[illegible]	[illegible]
[illegible]	[illegible]	[illegible]	[illegible]	[illegible]	[illegible]	[illegible]	[illegible]	[illegible]	[illegible]	[illegible]	[illegible]	[illegible]	[illegible]	[illegible]	[illegible]	[illegible]	[illegible]	[illegible]	[illegible]	[illegible]	[illegible]	[illegible]	[illegible]	[illegible]
[illegible]	[illegible]	[illegible]	[illegible]	[illegible]	[illegible]	[illegible]	[illegible]	[illegible]	[illegible]	[illegible]	[illegible]	[illegible]	[illegible]	[illegible]	[illegible]	[illegible]	[illegible]	[illegible]	[illegible]	[illegible]	[illegible]	[illegible]	[illegible]	[illegible]
[illegible]	[illegible]	[illegible]	[illegible]	[illegible]	[illegible]	[illegible]	[illegible]	[illegible]	[illegible]	[illegible]	[illegible]	[illegible]	[illegible]	[illegible]	[illegible]	[illegible]	[illegible]	[illegible]	[illegible]	[illegible]	[illegible]	[illegible]	[illegible]	[illegible]
[illegible]	[illegible]	[illegible]	[illegible]	[illegible]	[illegible]	[illegible]	[illegible]	[illegible]	[illegible]	[illegible]	[illegible]	[illegible]	[illegible]	[illegible]	[illegible]	[illegible]	[illegible]	[illegible]	[illegible]	[illegible]	[illegible]	[illegible]	[illegible]	[illegible]
[illegible]	[illegible]	[illegible]	[illegible]	[illegible]	[illegible]	[illegible]	[illegible]	[illegible]	[illegible]	[illegible]	[illegible]	[illegible]	[illegible]	[illegible]	[illegible]	[illegible]	[illegible]	[illegible]	[illegible]	[illegible]	[illegible]	[illegible]	[illegible]	[illegible]
[illegible]	Sligo	[illegible]	[illegible]	[illegible]	[illegible]	[illegible]	[illegible]	[illegible]	[illegible]	[illegible]	[illegible]	[illegible]	[illegible]	[illegible]	[illegible]	[illegible]	[illegible]	[illegible]	[illegible]	[illegible]	[illegible]	[illegible]	[illegible]	[illegible]
[illegible]	[illegible]	[illegible]	[illegible]	[illegible]	[illegible]	[illegible]	[illegible]	[illegible]	[illegible]	[illegible]	[illegible]	[illegible]	[illegible]	[illegible]	[illegible]	[illegible]	[illegible]	[illegible]	[illegible]	[illegible]	[illegible]	[illegible]	[illegible]	[illegible]
[illegible]	[illegible]	[illegible]	[illegible]	[illegible]	[illegible]	[illegible]	[illegible]	[illegible]	[illegible]	[illegible]	[illegible]	[illegible]	[illegible]	[illegible]	[illegible]	[illegible]	[illegible]	[illegible]	[illegible]	[illegible]	[illegible]	[illegible]	[illegible]	[illegible]
[illegible]	[illegible]	[illegible]	[illegible]	[illegible]	[illegible]	[illegible]	[illegible]	[illegible]	[illegible]	[illegible]	[illegible]	[illegible]	[illegible]	[illegible]	[illegible]	[illegible]	[illegible]	[illegible]	[illegible]	[illegible]	[illegible]	[illegible]	[illegible]	[illegible]
[illegible]	[illegible]	[illegible]	[illegible]	[illegible]	[illegible]	[illegible]	[illegible]	[illegible]	[illegible]	[illegible]	[illegible]	[illegible]	[illegible]	[illegible]	[illegible]	[illegible]	[illegible]	[illegible]	[illegible]	[illegible]	[illegible]	[illegible]	[illegible]	[illegible]
[illegible]	[illegible]	[illegible]	[illegible]	[illegible]	[illegible]	[illegible]	[illegible]	[illegible]	[illegible]	[illegible]	[illegible]	[illegible]	[illegible]	[illegible]	[illegible]	[illegible]	[illegible]	[illegible]	[illegible]	[illegible]	[illegible]	[illegible]	[illegible]	[illegible]
[illegible]	[illegible]	[illegible]	[illegible]	[illegible]	[illegible]	[illegible]	[illegible]	[illegible]	[illegible]	[illegible]	[illegible]	[illegible]	[illegible]	[illegible]	[illegible]	[illegible]	[illegible]	[illegible]	[illegible]	[illegible]	[illegible]	[illegible]	[illegible]	[illegible]
[illegible]	[illegible]	[illegible]	[illegible]	[illegible]	[illegible]	[illegible]	[illegible]	[illegible]	[illegible]	[illegible]	[illegible]	[illegible]	[illegible]	[illegible]	[illegible]	[illegible]	[illegible]	[illegible]	[illegible]	[illegible]	[illegible]	[illegible]	[illegible]	[illegible]
[illegible]	[illegible]	[illegible]	[illegible]	[illegible]	[illegible]	[illegible]	[illegible]	[illegible]	[illegible]	[illegible]	[illegible]	[illegible]	[illegible]	[illegible]	[illegible]	[illegible]	[illegible]	[illegible]	[illegible]	[illegible]	[illegible]	[illegible]	[illegible]	[illegible]
[illegible]	[illegible]	[illegible]	[illegible]	[illegible]	[illegible]	[illegible]	[illegible]	[illegible]	[illegible]	[illegible]	[illegible]	[illegible]	[illegible]	[illegible]	[illegible]	[illegible]	[illegible]	[illegible]	[illegible]	[illegible]	[illegible]	[illegible]	[illegible]	[illegible]
[illegible]	[illegible]	[illegible]	[illegible]	[illegible]	[illegible]	[illegible]	[illegible]	[illegible]	[illegible]	[illegible]	[illegible]	[illegible]	[illegible]	[illegible]	[illegible]	[illegible]	[illegible]	[illegible]	[illegible]	[illegible]	[illegible]	[illegible]	[illegible]	[illegible]
			[illegible]	[illegible]	[illegible]	[illegible]	[illegible]	[illegible]	[illegible]	[illegible]	[illegible]	[illegible]	[illegible]	[illegible]	[illegible]	[illegible]	[illegible]	[illegible]	[illegible]	[illegible]	[illegible]	[illegible]	[illegible]	

APPENDIX, No. 3.
Abstract of By-Laws, Orders, &c.

APPENDIX, No. 3.

ABSTRACT of BY-LAWS, ORDERS, &c., in force on 1st January, 1879, relating to the *Sea and Oyster* FISHERIES of IRELAND.

Place affected by By-Law and Date thereof.	Nature of By-Law.
	TRAWLING.
DUBLIN BAY, (10th Oct., 1842.)	Prohibiting Trawling inside lines drawn from the Bailey Light-house at Howth, to the Easternmost point of the rocks called the "Muglins;" thence by a straight line to the Southern point of Dalkey Island, thence by a straight line across Dalkey Sound, in the direction of the signal station on Killiney Hill.
EAST COAST, (18th Feb., 1851.)	Prohibiting Trawling within a line drawn from the Nose of Howth, to the Eastern point of St. Patrick's Island (Skerries), thence to Clogher Head; thence to Dunany Point; thence to Cranfield Point, in the County Down.
DUNDRUM BAY, &c., (3rd Dec., 1851.)	Prohibiting Trawling from Ballyhunter Rock, off Cranfield Point, to St. John's Point, both in the County Down.
BELFAST LOUGH, (27th Nov., 1869.)	Prohibiting Trawling in that part of said Lough of Belfast comprised within a straight line drawn from the Castle of Carrickfergus, in the County of the Town of Carrickfergus, to Rockport, in the County of Down, between the hours of Six o'Clock in the Evening and Six o'Clock in the Morning, during the Months of December, January, and February.
DONEGAL BAY, (16th Feb., 1857.)	Prohibiting Trawling within a straight line from the Bann Rock, to a place called Doorin Point.
GALWAY BAY, (5th Jan., 1851.)	When large shoals of Herrings shall have set in in the Bay, and while Boats are engaged in Drifting for Herrings or Mackerel, and when Boats shall commence Fishing for Herrings or Mackerel, that Trawl Boats shall keep at a distance of three miles from them.
(31st Aug., 1877.)	Repealing By-Law, dated 22nd March, 1843, prohibiting Trawling at all times within a straight line drawn from Barna Pier on the north to Glennagh Castle on the south side of said bay.
BRANDON BAY, (21st Aug., 1860.)	Prohibiting Trawling within a line drawn from Brandon Point to Cloghane.
BANTRY BAY, (17th March, 1856.)	Prohibiting Trawling within a straight line from Crowdy Point to Carrigaheve Rock, and from thence to Roancarrig Point, on the North Shore of Whiddy Island.
(11th Sept., 1861.)	And Prohibiting Trawling between sunset and sunrise."
WATERFORD HARBOUR, (18th Dec., 1873.)	Prohibiting Trawling by Boats exceeding ten tons measurement, within a line drawn from Coalpit Cottage, County Waterford, to Broomhill Point, County Wexford.
WEXFORD COAST, (20th April, 1842.)	Prohibiting Trawling in all places where there are Boats engaged in Herring or Mackerel Drift Net Fishing, and that Trawl Boats shall keep at a distance of at least three miles from all Boats fishing for Herrings or Mackerel, with Drift Nets. And whenever Herring or Mackerel Boats shall commence Drift Net Fishing in any place on or off the Coast of Wexford, the Trawl Boats shall depart therefrom, and keep at least three miles distant from the Drift Net Herring or Mackerel Boats.
	TRAMMEL NETS.
DUNGARVAN BAY, (6th July, 1848.)	Prohibiting the use of Trammel and every other Fixed or Moored Net (except Bag or other Nets for the taking of Salmon) in Dungarvan Bay, within the limit formed as follows, namely, the space lying between a line passing due East and West, through the Northernmost point of Helvick Head, and a line passing due East and West through the Southernmost point of Ballynacourty Head, in the Co. Waterford; but to the North and East of the line through Ballynacourty Head, and to the South and West of the line through Helvick Head, such Trammel or Moored Nets may be set, and remain set in the water from Three o'Clock, p.m., of one day, until Nine o'Clock, a.m., in the following day, during January, March, October, November, and December in each Year; and from Five o'Clock, p.m., of one day, to Seven o'Clock, a.m., in the following day, during
DUNGARVAN BAY, &c., &c. —continued.	May, June, July, August, and September. Also prohibiting such Nets athwart or within 200 yards of any boat, which at the time of setting such net shall be moored, and the Crew thereof engaged in Line Fishing, and to every train of such Trammel or Moored Nets shall be attached at least one floating buoy or board, upon which shall be painted in legible characters not less than one inch in length, in white upon a black ground, the Letter of the District, and the name of the Owner to which such Net belongs.
INVER BAY, (24th Sept., 1866.)	Prohibiting the use of Trammel Nets within or to the North east of a line drawn from the Mouth of the Bunlaghy River to Doorin Point.
KENMARE RIVER ESTUARY, (31st Dec., 1864.)	Permitting within the Estuary of the Kenmare River, in the County of Kerry, and eastward of a line drawn from the western point of Lamb's Head to the western point of Cod's Head, the use of Trammel and other Moored Nets for the capture of Sea Fish, from the hour of Three o'Clock in the Afternoon of any one day to the hour of Nine o'Clock in the Morning of the day next following, during the months of October, November, December, January, February, and March, in each year; and from the hour of Five o'Clock in the Afternoon of any one day to the hour of Seven o'Clock in the Morning of the day following, during the months of April, May, June, July, August, and September.
	GENERAL.
DROGHEDA & DUNDALK DISTRICTS (East Coast), (22nd Oct., 1873.)	Prohibiting use of Draw or Wade Nets with Meshes less than three and a half inches for capture of Fish between Bra Head and mouth of Annagassan River.
DUNDALK DISTRICT, STRANGFORD LOUGH, (1st Dec., 1873.)	Prohibiting use of Poke Nets for capture of Fish inside a line drawn across said Lough, from Mullog Point on the west to Ballyquintin Point on the east, between the last day of January and first day of November in each year.
SEA COAST, COUNTY DONEGAL, (30th Jan., 1874.)	Prohibiting use of Draw or Wade Nets for capture of Fish between Dunaff Head and Dunmore Head, and tidal parts of rivers flowing into the sea between said points and around the shores of Inishtrahull.
DONEGAL BAY, (21st April, 1874.)	Repealing By-law of 24th February, 1860, prohibiting use of Nets with Meshes less than one inch for capture of Fish of any kind on that part of the coast of the County Donegal inside or to the north-east and north of lines drawn from Rossan Point to Teelin Head, and from Teelin Head to Carrigan Head, and from Carrigan Head to Muckross Point, all in the Barony of Bannagh and County of Donegal.
	OYSTERS.
SOUTH-EAST COAST of IRELAND from WICKLOW HEAD to CARNSORE POINT, (1st Sept., 1868.)	That the Close Time, during which it shall not be lawful to dredge for, take, catch, or destroy any Oysters or Oyster Brood, on or off the South-east coast of Ireland, between Wicklow Head and Carnsore Point, shall be between the 30th April and the 1st September in each year.
COASTS of DUBLIN, WICKLOW, and WEXFORD, (23rd April, 1869.) Approved by Her Majesty in Council, 28th April, 1869.	Prohibiting between the 30th April and 1st September in each year the dredging for, taking, catching, or destroying any Oyster or Oyster Brood on or off any part of the East and South-East Coast of Ireland, within the distance of Twenty Miles measured from a straight line drawn from the Eastern point of Lambay Island, in the County Dublin, to Carnsore Point, in the County Wexford, outside the exclusive Fishery Limits of the British Islands.
WEXFORD COAST, (8th April, 1862.)	First.—All persons engaged in fishing for or taking Oysters off the said Wexford Coast, south of Raven Point, shall cull all such Oysters as may be taken or caught; and shall not remove from any Fishing Ground or Oyster Bed any Oyster of less dimensions than three inches, at the greatest diameter thereof, and shall un-

APPENDIX, No. 3.
Abstract of By-Laws, Orders, &c.

APPENDIX, No. 3—*continued.*

ABSTRACT of BY-LAWS, ORDERS, &c., in force on 1st January, 1879, relating to the *Sea and Oyster* FISHERIES of IRELAND.

Place affected by By-Law, and Date thereof	Nature of By-Law.
WEXFORD COAST, &c.—*continued.*	mediately throw back into the Sea all Oysters of less dimensions than aforesaid, as well as all gravel and fragments of shells as shall be raised or taken while engaged in such fishing; and no person shall take from any Oyster Bed, Rock, Strand, or Shore, of said Wexford Coast, south of Raven Point, any Oyster of less dimensions than three inches, at the greatest diameter thereof; and any person offending in any respect against this By-Law, Rule, or Regulation shall, for each offence, forfeit and pay a sum of Two Pounds. Second.—All persons are prohibited from throwing into the Sea, on any Oyster Bed, or Oyster Fishing Ground off the said Wexford Coast, the ballast of any boat, or any other matter or thing injurious or detrimental to the Oyster Fishery; and all persons acting contrary hereto shall, for each offence, forfeit and pay a sum of Two Pounds.
CORK HARBOUR, (29th Feb., 1876.)	First.—That between the 1st day of May and the 1st day of September in any year, no boat shall have on board any dredge or other implement for the taking of Oysters; and if, between the periods aforesaid, there shall be on board any boat in said Cork Harbour and the Estuaries of the Rivers flowing into same, any such dredge or other implement for the taking of Oysters, the master or owner of such boat shall, for each such offence, forfeit and pay a sum of Two Pounds. Second.—All persons engaged in fishing for or taking Oysters shall cull all such Oysters as may be taken or caught; and shall not remove from any Fishing Ground or Oyster Bed, any Oyster of less dimensions than two inches and one half at the greatest diameter thereof; and shall immediately throw back into the water all Oysters of less dimensions than aforesaid, as well as all gravel and fragments of shells as shall be raised or taken while engaged in such fishing; and no person shall take from any rock, strand, bed, or shore of said Cork Harbour and the Estuaries of the Rivers flowing into same, by any means whatsoever, any Oyster of less dimensions than two inches and one-half, at the greatest diameter thereof; nor sell, expose for sale, give, transfer, or purchase, receive, carry, or have in his or her custody or possession any such Oysters so taken, and any person offending in any respect against this By-Law, Rule, or Regulation shall, for each offence, forfeit and pay a sum of Five Pounds. Third.—All persons are prohibited from throwing into the Water, on any Oyster Bed or Oyster Fishing Ground in said Cork Harbour or the Estuaries of the Rivers flowing into same, the ballast of any boat, or any other matter or thing injurious or detrimental to the Oyster Fishery; and all persons acting contrary hereto shall, for each offence, forfeit and pay a sum of Two Pounds. Fourth.—No person shall, between Sunset and Sunrise, dredge for, take, or catch any Oysters in said Cork Harbour or the Estuaries of the Rivers flowing into same; and every person acting contrary hereto shall, for each offence forfeit and pay a sum of Five Pounds.
KINSALE HARBOUR and BANDON RIVER, (22nd August, 1872.)	That all persons fishing for or taking Oysters in any part of the Fishing Grounds or Oyster Beds situated in Kinsale Harbour and Bandon River, in the County of Cork, shall cull all such Oysters as may be taken or caught, and shall not remove from such Fishing Grounds or Oyster Beds any Oyster of less dimensions than three inches at the greatest diameter thereof, but shall immediately throw back into the water all Oysters of less dimensions than aforesaid; and any person offending in any respect against this By-Law shall for each such offence forfeit and pay a sum of Two Pounds.
TRALEE BAY, (7th Aug., 1872.)	That the Close Time during which it shall not be lawful to dredge for, take, catch, or destroy any Oysters or Oyster Brood within said Tralee Bay, or off or from any of the shores or rocks thereof shall be between the 15th day of March and the 1st day of November in each year.
(29th Feb., 1876.)	First.—That during the Close Season for Oysters in the said Bay of Tralee, no boat, in the said Bay of Tralee, shall have on board any dredge or other implement for the taking of Oysters; and if, during the period aforesaid, there shall be on board any boat any such dredge or other implement for the taking of Oysters, the master or owner of such boat shall, for each such offence, forfeit and pay a sum of Two Pounds. Second.—All persons engaged in fishing for or taking Oysters in said Bay of Tralee, shall cull all such Oysters as may be taken or caught; and shall not remove from any Fishing Ground or Oyster Bed any Oyster of less dimensions than two inches and one-half at the greatest diameter thereof, and shall immediately throw back into the Sea all Oysters of less dimensions than aforesaid, as well as all gravel and fragments of shells as shall be raised or taken while engaged in such fishing, and no person shall take from any rock, strand, or shore of said Bay of Tralee, by any means whatsoever, any Oyster of less dimensions than two inches and one-half, at the greatest diameter thereof; nor sell, expose for sale, give, transfer, or purchase, receive, carry, or have in his or her custody or possession, any such Oysters so taken; and any person offending in any respect against this By-Law, Rule, or Regulation shall, for each offence, forfeit and pay a sum of Two Pounds.
RIVER SHANNON, &c. (29th Feb., 1876.)	First.—That during the Close Season for Oysters, which is between the 1st May and 1st September in the said River Shannon, or in any of the Bays or Inlets thereof, no boat, in the said River Shannon, or in any of the Bays or Inlets thereof, shall have on board any dredge or other implement for the taking of Oysters; and if, during the period aforesaid, there shall be on board any boat any such dredge or other implement for the taking of Oysters, the master or owner of such boat shall, for each such offence, forfeit and pay a sum of Two Pounds. Second.—All persons engaged in fishing for or taking Oysters in said River Shannon, or in any of the Bays or Inlets thereof, shall cull all such Oysters as may be taken or caught, and shall not remove from any Fishing Ground or Oyster Bed any oyster of less dimensions than two inches and one-half at the greatest diameter thereof, and shall immediately throw back into the water all Oysters of less dimensions than aforesaid, as well as all gravel and fragments of shells as shall be raised or taken while engaged in such fishing; and no person shall take from any Rock, Strand, or Shore of said River Shannon, or of any of the Bays or Inlets thereof, by any means whatsoever, any Oyster of less dimensions than two inches and one-half at the greatest diameter thereof; nor sell, expose for sale, give, transfer, or purchase, receive, carry, or have in his or her custody or possession any such Oysters so taken; and any person offending in any respect against this By-Law, Rule, or Regulation shall, for each offence, forfeit and pay a sum of Two Pounds. Third.—All persons are hereby prohibited from throwing into the water, on any Oyster Bed or Oyster Fishing Ground in said River Shannon, or in any of the Bays or Inlets thereof as aforesaid, the ballast of any boat, or any other matter or thing injurious or detrimental to the Oyster Fishery; and all persons acting contrary hereto shall, for each offence, forfeit and pay a sum of Two Pounds. Fourth.—No person shall, between sunset and sunrise, dredge for, take, or catch, any Oysters within said River Shannon, or within any of the Bays or Inlets thereof as aforesaid; and every person acting contrary hereto shall, for each offence, forfeit and pay a sum of Two Pounds.
GALWAY BAY, (13th August, 1877.)	That the Close Time during which it shall not be lawful to dredge for, take, catch, or destroy by any means whatsoever any Oysters or Oyster Brood on or off the Public or Natural Oyster Beds within said Galway Bay, or in any of the Bays or Inlets thereof, or off or from any of the shores or rocks thereof, shall be between the 1st day of January and the 30th day of November in each year, both said days inclusive.
(5th Nov., 1877.)	First.—It shall not be lawful for any person to dredge for, take, or catch any Oysters in Galway Bay, or in any of the Bays or Inlets thereof, between the 1st day of January and

APPENDIX, No. 3. Abstract of By-Laws, Orders, &c.

APPENDIX, No. 3—*continued.*

ABSTRACT of BY-LAWS, ORDERS, &c., in force on 1st January, 1879, relating to the *Sea and Oyster* FISHERIES of IRELAND.

Place affected by By-Law, and Date thereof.	Nature of By-Law.
GALWAY BAY.—*continued.*	the 30th day of November in each year, both said days inclusive, being the Close Season for Oysters in the said Bay, Bays, and Inlets, or between Sunset and Sunrise at any Season of the year; and any person offending against this By-Law, Rule, or Regulation shall, for each such offence, forfeit and pay a sum of Three Pounds. Second.—No Boat, in Galway Bay, or in any of the Bays or Inlets thereof, shall, between the 1st day of January and the 30th day of November in each year, both said days inclusive, have on board any dredge or other implement for the taking of Oysters; and the master or owner of such boat shall, for each such offence, forfeit and pay a sum of Three Pounds. Third.—All persons engaged in fishing for or taking Oysters in said Galway Bay, or in any of the Bays or Inlets thereof, shall, immediately on any Oysters being brought on board any boat, cull all such Oysters as may be taken or caught, and shall immediately throw back into the water all Oysters of less dimensions than three inches at the greatest diameter thereof, as well as all gravel and fragments of shells raised or taken while engaged in such fishing; and shall not remove from any Fishing Ground or Oyster Bed any Oyster of less dimensions than three inches at the greatest diameter thereof; and no person shall pick, gather, or take from any rock, strand, or shore of Galway Bay, or of any of the Bays or Inlets thereof, by any means whatsoever, any Oyster of less dimensions than three inches at the greatest diameter thereof, nor sell, expose for sale, give, transfer, or purchase, receive, carry, or have in his or her custody or possession any Oysters of less dimensions than aforesaid, and any person offending in any respect against this By-Law, Rule, or Regulation shall, for each offence, forfeit and pay a sum of Two Pounds.
CLEW BAY, ACHILL SOUND, BLACKSOD and BROADHAVEN BAYS and the Bays connected therewith. (12th April, 1877.)	Prohibiting for three years from the 1st October, 1877, the dredging for, taking, catching, or destroying, by any means whatsoever, any Oyster or Oyster Brood in any part of the said Clew Bay, Achill Sound, Blacksod and Broadhaven Bays, or in any of the Bays or Inlets thereof. And any person dredging for, taking, catching, or destroying, by any means whatsoever, any Oysters or Oyster Brood in said Bays or Inlets contrary hereto, during the period aforesaid, shall, for each offence, forfeit and pay a penalty of Five Pounds. "During the period aforesaid, no Boat shall have on board any dredge or other implement for the taking of Oysters in the said Clew Bay, Achill Sound, Blacksod and Broadhaven Bays, and the Bays or Inlets connected therewith; and if, during the period aforesaid, there shall be on board any Boat any such dredge or other implement for the taking of Oysters, the master or owner of such boat shall, for each such offence, forfeit and pay a sum of Two Pounds."
SLIGO, BALLISODARE, and DRUMCLIFFE BAYS (29th April, 1878.)	First.—That during the Close Season for Oysters in the said Sligo, Ballisodare, and Drumcliffe Bays, which is between 1st May and 1st September, no boat, in the said Sligo, Ballisodare, and Drumcliffe Bays, shall have on board any dredge or other implement for the taking of Oysters, and if, during the Close Season aforesaid, there shall be on board any boat any such dredge or other implement for the taking of Oysters, the master or owner of such boat shall, for each such offence, forfeit and pay a sum of Two Pounds. Second.—All persons engaged in fishing for or taking Oysters in said Sligo, Ballisodare, and Drumcliffe Bays, shall cull all such Oysters as may be taken or caught, and shall not remove from any Fishing Ground or Oyster Bed any Oyster of less dimensions than two inches and one-half, at the greatest diameter thereof, and shall immediately throw back into the water all oysters of less dimensions than aforesaid, as well as all gravel and fragments of shells as shall be raised or taken while engaged in such fishing; and no person shall take from any Rock, Strand, or Shore of said
SLIGO, &c.—*continued.*	Sligo, Ballisodare, and Drumcliffe Bays, by any means whatsoever, any Oyster of less dimensions than two inches and one-half, at the greatest diameter thereof, nor sell, expose for sale, give, transfer, or purchase, receive, carry, or have in his or her custody or possession any such Oysters so taken; and any person offending in any respect against this By-Law, Rule, or Regulation shall, for each offence, forfeit and pay a sum of Two Pounds. Third.—All persons are hereby prohibited from throwing into the water on any Oyster Bed, or Oyster Fishing Ground in said Sligo, Ballisodare, and Drumcliffe Bays, the ballast of any boat, or any other matter or thing injurious or detrimental to the Oyster Fishery; and all persons acting contrary hereto shall, for each offence, forfeit and pay a sum of Two Pounds. Fourth.—Every dredge or other implement for the taking of Oysters shall have a number corresponding with the number of the boat on which it is employed, or to which it belongs, stamped thereon, and all persons acting contrary hereto shall, for each offence, forfeit and pay a sum of Two Pounds.
LOUGH SWILLY, &c., &c. (18th Feb., 1878.)	First.—That during the Close Season for Oysters in the said Lough Swilly, or in any of the Bays, Creeks, or Inlets thereof (which is between 1st May and 1st September), no boat, in the said Lough Swilly, or in any of the Bays, Creeks, or Inlets thereof, shall have on board any dredge or other implement for the taking of Oysters; and if, during the period aforesaid, there shall be on board any boat any such dredge or other implement for the taking of Oysters, the master or owner of such boat shall, for each such offence, forfeit and pay a sum of Two Pounds. Second.—All persons engaged in fishing for or taking Oysters in said Lough Swilly, or in any of the Bays, Creeks, or Inlets thereof, shall cull all such Oysters as may be taken or caught; and shall not remove from any Fishing Ground or Oyster Bed any Oyster of less dimensions than two inches and one-half at the greatest diameter thereof; and shall immediately throw back into the sea all Oysters of less dimensions than aforesaid, as well as all gravel and fragments of shells as shall be raised or taken while engaged in such fishing, and no person shall take from any Rock, Strand, or Shore of said Lough Swilly, or of any of the Bays, Creeks, or Inlets thereof, by any means whatsoever, any Oyster of less dimensions than two inches and one-half at the greatest diameter thereof, nor sell, expose for sale, give, transfer, or purchase, receive, carry, or have in his or her custody or possession any such Oysters of less dimensions than aforesaid; and any person offending in any respect against this By-Law, Rule, or Regulation shall, for each offence, forfeit and pay a sum of Two Pounds. Third.—All persons are hereby prohibited from throwing into the water, on any Oyster Bed, or Oyster Fishing Ground, in said Lough Swilly, or in any of the Bays, Creeks, or Inlets thereof as aforesaid, the ballast of any boat, or any other matter or thing injurious or detrimental to the Oyster Fishery; and all persons acting contrary hereto shall, for each offence, forfeit and pay a sum of Two Pounds.
STRANGFORD LOUGH (13th Nov., 1877.)	That the Close Time during which it shall not be lawful to dredge for, take, catch, or destroy by any means whatsoever any Oysters or Oyster Brood on or off the Public or Natural Oyster Beds within said Strangford Lough, or off or from any of the shores or rocks thereof, shall be between the 1st day of March and the 31st day of August in each year, both said days inclusive.
(31st Dec. 1877.)	First.—Between the first day of March and the first day of September in any year, thus being the close time within which it is not lawful to dredge for, take, catch, or destroy any Oyster or Oyster Brood in Strangford Lough, no boat in Strangford Lough shall have on board any dredge or other implement for the taking of Oysters; and if, between the periods aforesaid, there shall be on board any boat any such

APPENDIX No. 3—*continued.*

Appendix No. 3. Abstract of By-Laws, Orders, &c.

ABSTRACT of BY-LAWS, ORDERS, &c., in force on 1st January, 1878, relating to the *Sea and Oyster* FISHERIES of IRELAND.

Place affected by By-Law, and Date thereof.	Nature of By-Law.	Place affected by By-Law, and Date thereof.	Nature of By-Law.
STRANGFORD LOUGH—*continued.*	dredge or other implement for the taking of Oysters, the master or owner of such boat shall, for each such offence, forfeit and pay a sum of Two Pounds. Second.—All persons engaged in fishing for or taking Oysters in Strangford Lough shall, immediately on any Oysters being brought on board any boat, cull all such Oysters as may be taken or caught; and shall not remove from any fishing ground or oyster bed any Oyster of less dimensions than two inches and one-half at the greatest diameter thereof, and shall immediately throw back into the sea all Oysters of less dimensions than aforesaid, as well as all gravel and fragments of shells raised or taken in such fishing, and no person shall take from any rock, strand or shore of Strangford Lough, by any means whatsoever, any Oyster of less dimensions than two inches and one-half at the greatest diameter thereof; and no person shall sell, expose for sale, give, transfer or purchase, receive, carry, or have in his or her custody or possession, any such Oysters so taken; and any person offending in any respect against this by-law, rule, or regulation shall, for each offence, forfeit and pay a sum of Two Pounds. Third.—No person shall, between sunset and sunrise, dredge for, take, or catch, any Oysters within Strangford Lough aforesaid; and every person acting contrary hereto shall, for each offence, forfeit and pay a sum of Two Pounds.	CARLINGFORD LOUGH—*con.* (24th Nov., 1877.)	First.—Between the first day of March and the first day of November in any year, that being the close time within which it is not lawful to dredge for, take, catch, or destroy any Oyster or Oyster Brood in Carlingford Lough, no boat in Carlingford Lough shall have on board any Dredge or other Implement for the taking of Oysters; and if, between the periods aforesaid, there shall be on board any boat any such Dredge or other implement for the taking of Oysters, the master or owner of such boat shall, for each such offence, forfeit and pay a sum of Two Pounds. Second.—All persons engaged in fishing for or taking Oysters in Carlingford Lough shall, immediately on any Oysters being taken, cull all such Oysters as may be taken or caught; and shall immediately throw back into the sea all Oysters of less dimensions than two inches and one-half at the greatest diameter thereof, as well as all gravel and fragments of shells raised or taken in such fishing; and shall not remove from any fishing ground or oyster bed any Oyster of less dimensions than two inches and one-half at the greatest diameter thereof; and no person shall take from any rock, strand, or shore of Carlingford Lough, by any means whatsoever, any Oyster of less dimensions than two inches and one-half at the greatest diameter thereof; and no person shall sell, expose for sale, give, transfer or purchase, receive, carry or have in his or her custody or possession any Oysters of less dimensions than aforesaid so taken; and any person offending in any respect against this bye-law, rule, or regulation shall, for each offence, forfeit and pay a sum of Two Pounds. Third.—No person shall, between sunset and sunrise, dredge for, take, or catch, any Oysters within Carlingford Lough aforesaid; and every person acting contrary hereto shall, for each offence, forfeit and pay a sum of Two Pounds.
CARLINGFORD LOUGH. (21st June, 1877.)	Prohibiting at any time after the 1st day of November, 1877, to use for the taking of Oysters in any part of Carlingford Lough, in either of the counties of Louth and Down respectively, the instrument commonly called and known as the grape, or any other instrument or device of the like construction or nature. Any person offending against this By-Law shall forfeit and pay for each offence the sum of Four Pounds, and every such grape, or other instrument or device which shall be used contrary to this By-Law, shall be forfeited.		

APPENDIX, No. 4.

Appendix No. 4.

LIST of OYSTER LICENCES REVOKED up to date of this Report.

Date of Licence.	Persons to whom granted.	Locality of Beds.	No. of Acres.	Date of Revocation.
County Cork.				
1867. 27th August,	Thomas Eccles,	Glengarriff Harbour,	9	21st October, 1876.
1867. 10th July,	M. J. C. Longfield,	Roaringwater Bay,	310	7th March, 1877.
1869. 13th February,	Earl of Bantry,	Adrigole Harbour,	16	9th March, 1878.
1869. 15th March,	John Warren Payne,	Bantry Bay,	51	19th October, 1876
1871. 22nd March,	Earl of Bantry and T. J. Leahy,	Berehaven,	129	15th March, 1878
County Kerry.				
1860. 3rd February,	Knight of Kerry,	Valencia Harbour,	78	8th March, 1878.
1867. 10th July,	Thomas Sandes,	River Shannon,	790	28th October, 1876.
1869. 13th February,	Henry Herbert,	Kenmare Bay,	20	25th May, 1877.
1871. 27th March,	Earl of Bantry,	Ardgroom Harbour,	240	16th December, 1876.
County Galway.				
1864. 31st October,	R. E. Lynch Athy,	Galway Bay,	100	20th March, 1876.
1864. 31st October,	P. M. Lynch,	Do.,	320	26th April, 1877.
1864. 31st December,	T. Young Prior,	Ballinakill Harbour,	20	18th June, 1878.
1865. 1st December,	Captain Acheson,	Do.,	18	10th April, 1878.
1865. 1st December,	Robert M'Keown,	Killary Bay,	81	10th April, 1876.
1867. 10th July,	William and James St. George,	Galway Bay,	810	26th January, 1878.
1867. 10th July,	Christopher T. Redington,	Do.	650	29th March, 1876.
County Mayo.				
1865. 13th April,	Marquess of Sligo,	Clew Bay,	190	26th October, 1876.
1865. 2nd November,	Law Life Assurance Society,	Do.,	718	11th January, 1877.
1865. 1st December,	Marquess of Sligo,	Do.,	26	9th October, 1878.
1866. 20th April,	Do.,	Do.,	270	9th October, 1876.
1869. 14th June,	William Little,	Killala Bay,	190	19th October, 1876.
1872. 16th December,	William O. M'Cormick,	Rathfran Bay,	95	16th January, 1877.
1873. 8th December,	Mary Fegan,	Clew Bay,	26	24th May, 1878.
County Antrim.				
1862. 3rd March,	James Walker,	Belfast Lough,	137	7th March, 1877
County Waterford.				
1864. 11th November,	John R. Dower,	Dungarvan Harbour,	27	22nd March, 1877.

APPENDIX,

LIST of LICENSES to Plant OYSTER BEDS *in force* on 31st December,

No. of License.	Date of License.	Persons to whom Granted.	Present Owner or Lessee.	Locality of Beds.	Area of Beds. A.	R.	P.	Average area of Beds available.
	County Dublin.				A.	R.	P.	Acres.
73	19th July, 1867,	Richard D. Kane,	Richard D Kane,	Howth Strand,	36	0	0	16
	County Wicklow.							
143	31st August, 1874,	Henry Pomeroy Truell,	Henry Pomeroy Truell,	Cloonmannon Lough,	63	1	30	
	County Wexford.							
82	20th April, 1868,	William Dargan,	John Hoey,	Wexford Harbour,	78	0	0	70
160	7th January, 1876,	Thomas J Hutchinson,	Thomas J. Hutchinson,	Duncormick Estuary,	11	3	31	
	County Waterford.							
30	6th March, 1862,	Edmund Power,	Edmund Power,	Tramore Bay,	370	0	0	108
33	2nd February, 1864,	Earl Fortescue,	Earl Fortescue,	Do.	33	0	0	
41	11th November, 1864,	A. Beale,	John Kendall,	Dungarvan Harbour,	85	0	0	
136	27th October, 1874,	John Kendall,	Do.,	Dungarvan Bay,	240	2	02	
	County Cork.							
4	24th February, 1846,	R T Evanson,	M. H. Morris,	Dunmanus Bay,	19	0	10	
16	20th July, 1846,	Lord Charles P. P. Clinton,	Lord Charles P.P. Clinton,	Bear Haven,	65	0	0	
24	4th October, 1864,	M C Cramer,	M C Cramer,	Oyster Haven,	20	0	0	
25	4th October, 1864,	Ebenezer Pike,	Ebenezer Pike,	Lough Mahon, Estuary of Lee,	47	0	0	
36	31st October, 1864,	Robert T. Atkins,	Robert T. Atkins,	Lough Hyne,	25	0	0	13
42	31st December, 1864,	Captain W. F. Barry,	Captain W. F. Barry,	Glandore Harbour,	88	0	0	88
46	2nd December, 1864,	Thomas M'Carthy Collins,	Thomas M'Carthy Collins,	Roaringwater Bay,	75	0	0	75
67	16th July, 1867,	Horatio H Townsend,	Horatio H Townsend,	Skull Harbour	230	0	0	
76	19th July, 1867,	Mrs Elizabeth Bury,	John O'Leary,	Lough Mahon,	78	0	0	20
77	Do.	John Smyth,	John Smyth,	Midleton River,	10	2	0	6
79	19th July, 1867,	Thomas Hicks,	Thomas Hicks,	Roaringwater Bay,	46	0	0	46
80	12th February, 1868,	Richard Lyons,	Richard Lyons,	Midleton River,	10	0	0	9
85	19th March, 1868,	Stephen Browne,	Stephen Browne,	Dunmanus Bay,	6	0	0	4
84	16th February, 1869,	Earl of Bantry,	Earl of Bantry,	Glengariffe Harbour,	65	0	0	20
85	14th June, 1869,	Mrs Catherine Bourne,	Mrs. Catherine Bourne,	Courtmacsherry Bay,	60	0	0	
106	27th March, 1871,	Thomas Hicks,	Thomas Hicks,	Roaringwater Bay,	30	0	0	
117	21st June, 1873,	Earl of Bandon,	Earl of Bandon,	Dunmanus Bay,	183	3	21	
118	14th October, 1873,	S. R. Townsend,	S. R. Townsend,	Ballydehob Harbour, Roaringwater Bay,	240	3	30	240
126	6th March, 1873,	Lt. Col Wm. H Longfield,	S A. Beamish,	Cork Harbour,	27	3	30	6
134	Do.	Thomas Hicks,	Thomas Hicks,	Roaringwater Bay,	145	0	30	
138	28th January, 1874,	Sir Henry W. Becher, bt.,	Sir Henry W. Becher, bt.,	Lough Hyne,	90	1	34	
146	27th December, 1874,	Standish D. O'Grady and Rev. R. H. Newenham,	Standish D. O'Grady and Rev. R. H. Newenham,	Owenboy River,	A 26	1	2	21
					B 36	2	16	24
	County Kerry.							
3	6th June, 1846,	F. H. Downing,	J Townsend Trench,	Off Dunrue Point,	5	2	32	6
5	6th February, 1861,	John Mahony,	Colonel Goff,	Estuary of Kenmare River,	108	2	0	108
8	Do.	Rev. Denis Mahony,	R. J. Mahony,	Do.	147	2	8	16-99
61	12th May, 1863,	Lord Baron Ventry,	Lord Baron Ventry,	Dingle Harbour,	130	0	0	
66	24th December, 1863,	Richard Mahony,	Richard Mahony,	Kenmare Estuary,	80	0	0	1

No. 5.

1878, and Substance of Reports received as to state of Beds.

No. of Licence.	Substance of Reports received as to state of Beds.
	County Dublin.
73	Purchased and put down over 8,303 full grown oysters. Sold 1,800 at about 10s. per hundred. No spat fallen, owing to tidal currents. No French oysters laid down. No general remarks.
	County Wicklow.
143	In consequence of ill-health was advised to spend the winter abroad, and was therefore unable to restock the bed since date of last report.
	County Wexford.
43	Nothing done since last report, embankment at Big Island not being completed.
150	No replies received.
	County Waterford.
60	Nothing done since last report. No oysters taken off, except a few for private use. None sold. Could not procure any brood oysters. No appearance of spat. Has always been of opinion that this bed is useless for breeding, but favourably situated for fattening. Hopes to be able to procure seed oysters from some natural bed.
38	Nothing done since last report. Beds in a very indifferent state, many oysters destroyed by inflow of sand. French oysters can hardly be said to have succeeded, though no very large proportion died in transit. A good many perished subsequently from various causes, and general result of experiment does not encourage a repetition on a larger scale.
41	No replies received.
106	Do.
	County Cork.
4	Nothing done since last report. States to clean the bed, lay and protect oysters, would require more care and capital than he could afford to give to it. Oysters appear to fatten well on it, but don't increase in number.
14	Bed cleared of weeds, mussels, &c. No oysters taken off, and none laid down. Noticed some spat, but not in large quantities. Is sorry to say bed is not in a good state. Is informed oysters are getting into deep waters. They are not increasing on the beds. Strongly suspects they are stolen. Has from time to time noticed that oysters are to be found in deep water, and thinks this attributable to the fresh water being forced into a particular channel. Has lately ordered embankment to be knocked down so that the fresh water may spread over the entire strand.
24	No replies received.
25	States it is useless to do anything to cultivate oysters until there is some simple way of protecting them from being stolen.
38	In consequence of illness is unable to attend to business.
42	Believes bed is most favourably circumstanced, but has not laid down any oysters, having ascertained that expense would be considerable. Would be glad to meet with any person disposed to stock bed.
45	Bed preserved. No oysters taken off or laid down. Being from home is unable to report as to fall of spat. A fair stock of oysters on at present, and if he can only succeed in preserving bed from being poached it will become valuable, as oysters thrive almost everywhere along the coast—that is when laid down in proper places.
67	Nothing done to this bed since last report.
75	Bed cleaned. About 25,400 oysters sold in 1878, and 100,000 laid down. Spat showed on only about 300 oysters. Beds in fair state. All oysters laid down were brought from France. About 1,900 oysters were lost in transit, owing to delay on arrival of steamer, bad packing, &c.
77	Beds cleared of mussels and weeds, and outer portion worked with dredge to stir and clear ground. 1,296 oysters sold. None laid down, but purposes laying down 50,000 in 1879. A fall of spat noticed every year, little of which comes to any use. Must be killed by crabs or other enemies. Beds fairly prosperous at present. Laid down 110,000 French oysters, which have succeeded very well. Few died in transit, except from actual injury. A number died afterwards, which cannot well be accounted for, but probably from the effects of the journey, as none appeared to have been forced, nor had those that died grown after being laid. If loans were made for the purpose of stocking oyster beds, to be repaid in three or four instalments, many would avail of it.
78	Nothing done since last report. No oysters sold. Is not aware of any fall of spat. Fears from roughness of channel shall have to wait a long time for success.
83	Bed kept clean, and replaced any oysters thrown out too far by wind and sea. Sold about 5,040 oysters in 1878. Did not lay down any. Some spat, but very inconsiderable. Bed in good condition, some small oysters doing well, and will be fit for market next year, in 1880. Has not laid down any French oysters since last report, but they have always been a great success with him. Only that his means are limited, and has met with reverses, would go in largely for them. There are very few lost in transit, say about 5 per hundred. Would advise anyone buying to get the larger size. The small ones did well with him, but took three years to become saleable. The large ones are fit to sell the year after bedding.
88	Has laid down a wooden frame to form a concrete fence to protect bed from swell of the Atlantic, but frame was carried away by the swell. Hopes to make experiment more successfully this spring. Laid down no oysters, fence not being completed. No fall of spat. Has laid down French oysters previous years.
85	No replies received.
86	Do.
105	Nothing done since last report. No oysters sold. No fall of spat noticed. No French oysters laid down.
117	Nothing done to bed since last report. No oysters sold, none laid down. No spat.
118	Nothing done since last report. Very little spat. Considerable quantity of small oysters on bed with small proportion of those once so plenty. No French oysters laid down. Had beds dredged and found oysters very little grown, although 2 years down, what were dredged were too small for sale.
138	No replies received.
174	Same replies as to license, No. 105.
139	Nothing done since last report. No oysters taken off or sold and none put down. No signs of spat. French oysters did not succeed, many died in transit and on the beds. Thinks there must be some vermin which attack the oysters, as there are numbers of double shells empty. The oysters still alive are increasing in size. Fears bed not well situated.
148	Over 61,000 French oysters laid down, and more ordered, but have not arrived, being delayed owing to the severity of the winter. No oysters sold. No fall of spat. Cannot report as to state of beds as they have not been tried since oysters laid down. The oysters arrived in good condition.
	County Kerry.
3	Nothing done since last report.
5	Bed allowed to rest since last report. No oysters taken off or sold. None put down. No appearance of spat. 10,000 French oysters were laid down but do not appear to have succeeded so far as increasing in number, but they did not die in transit. Beds appear to be suited only for fattening not for breeding, though some years ago they bred well.
8	Oysters previously planted saved, and collectors put down. About 2,000 sold, none planted in 1878. No appearance of spat. Does not consider oysters very promising. Cannot say that French oysters succeeded. A good many died in transit and on the beds.
31	Nothing done since last report, no oysters taken off. Intends laying down a large quantity of oysters on the bed.
50	Best spatting ground cleaned and vermin destroyed. No oysters taken off bed and none laid down. A slight fall of spat. Considers beds slowly improving.

Appendix, No. 5.

Appendix

LIST of LICENSES to Plant OYSTER BEDS *in force* on 31st December

No. of License	Date of License	Persons to whom Granted	Present Owner or Lessee	Locality of Beds	Area of Beds A.	R.	P.	Average area of Beds available
	County Kerry—*con.*				A.	R.	P.	Acres.
78	18th July, 1867,	Stephen E. Collis,	Stephen E. Collis,	River Shannon,	212	0	0	
94	11th February, 1868,	Charles Sandes,	Charles Sandes,	River Shannon,	58	0	0	13-25
61	21th March, 1866,	Richard J. Mahony,	Richard J. Mahony,	Kenmare Bay,	46	0	0	8
98	Do.	Thos. Kingston Sullivan,	Thos. Kingston Sullivan,	Do.	126	0	0	
128	14th June, 1872,	Robert M'Cowen,	Robert M'Cowen,	Barrow Harbour,	84	1	28	30
154	30th November, 1878,	Samuel T. Heard,	Samuel T. Heard,	Kenmare Bay,	62	0	17	
163	Do.	Do.	Do.	Do.	117	3	28	
	County Clare.							
26	14th February, 1862,	Robert W. C. Reeves,	Robert W. C. Reeves,	Clonderlaw Bay,	113	0	0	20
51	16th June, 1866,	Colonel C. M. Vandeleur,	Colonel C. M. Vandeleur,	Poulnasherry Bay,	100	0	0	12
84	16th July, 1867,	Robert W. C. Reeves,	Robert W. C. Reeves,	River Shannon,	80	0	0	25
	County Galway.							
12	14th November, 1864,	J. K. Botwell,	William Young,	Ballyconneely Bay,	223	0	0	20
16	21st August, 1866,	William Foreman,	John Kendall,	Ardbear Bay,	90	0	0	7
17	15th February, 1868,	Rev. A. Magee,	Rev. A. Magee,	Streamstown and Cleggan Bays.	277	0	0	10
18	Do.	A. C. Lambert,	A. C. Lambert,	Killary Harbour,	118	0	0	62
19	3rd February, 1864,	Rev. R. H. Wall,	Walter S. Wall,	Mannin & Ardbear Bays,	818	0	0	188
26	11th May, 1860,	Edward Browne,	Gillman Browne,	Ballinakill Harbour,	322	0	0	40
27	10th January, 1861,	William Forbes,	William Forbes,	Bertraghboy Bay,	225	0	0	
36	8th April, 1864,	Lord Wallscourt,	Lord Wallscourt,	Galway Bay,	1,770	0	0	308
37	1st October, 1864,	John Kendall,	John Kendall,	Ardbear & Mannin Bays,	236	0	0	10
46	31st December, 1864,	C. P. Archer,	Thomas Russell,	Ballinakill Harbour,	48	0	0	
40	Do.	P. Macauley,	Mitchell Henry, M.P.,	Ballinakill and Barnaderg Bays	140	0	0	120
81	24th July, 1867,	Francis J. Graham,	Francis J. Graham,	Barnaderg Bay,	90	0	0	1
90	4th March, 1869,	John P. Nolan,	John P. Nolan,	Ard Bay,	700	0	0	200
114	24th December, 1871,	Colin Hugh Thomson,	Colin Hugh Thomson,	Killary Bay,	201	2	0	50
118	9th February, 1872,	W. and J. St. George,	W. and J. St. George,	Galway Bay,	610	0	0	60
128	31st December, 1873,	Gillman Browne,	Gillman Browne,	Ballynakill Bay,	78	3	6	
130	10th April, 1874,	Rev. R. Gibbings, D.D.,	Rev. R. Gibbings, D.D.,	Kingstown Bay,	128	2	24	30
148	29th December, 1875,	Edmond O'Flaherty,	Edmond O'Flaherty,	Camus Bay,	107	2	29	
144	30th June, 1877,	Lord Wallscourt,	Lord Wallscourt,	Galway Bay,	153	2	5	
155	26th October, 1878,	Mitchell Henry,	Mitchell Henry,	Ballynakill Harbour,	400	0	0	
	County Mayo.							
1	5th November, 1846,	W. H. Carter,	W. H. Carter,	Trawmore Bay,	10	1	11	
8	17th November, 1862,	John C. Garvey,	Captain Geo. Austin,	Clew Bay,	100	3	32	44
11	24th November, 1864,	Hon. David Plunket,	James M'Donnell,	Killary Harbour,	288	0	0	
18	19th July, 1866,	John Richards,	John Richards,	Blacksod Bay,	80	0	0	8
21	3rd February, 1866,	Captain W. Houston,	William Barker,	Killary Harbour,	42	0	0	91
22	13th February, 1866,	William M'Cormick,	W. Dickens,	Achill Sound,	140	0	0	100
31	28th May, 1863,	George Clive,	Henry W. Birch,	Do.	480	0	0	8
36	18th June, 1864,	A. W. Wyndham,	Victor C. Kennedy,	Newport Bay,	60	0	0	10
66	28th September, 1866,	Captain George Austin,	Captain George Austin,	Westport Bay,	144	0	0	27
67	31st December, 1864,	Colonel F. A. K. Gore,	Sir Chas. A. Gore, bart.,	Killala Bay,	875	0	0	22
63	2nd November, 1865,	Marquess of Sligo,	Marquess of Sligo,	Clew Bay,	96	0	0	21
64	1st December, 1858,	Most Rev. Dr. M'Hale,	Rev. Thomas M'Hale, Rev. Canon Bourke, Rev. James M'Gee, trustees	Shores of Achill Island,	135	0	0	31
84	21st April, 1866,	Miss Anne Fowler,	Henry James F. Moran,	Blacksod Bay,	31	0	0	1
69	16th July, 1867,	Mrs. Elisabeth Atkinson,	J. Gallagher,	Broadhaven Bay,	100	0	0	13-21

No. 5—*continued.*

1878, and Substance of Reports received as to state of Beds—*continued.*

No. of License.	Substance of Reports received as to state of Beds.
	County Kerry—*continued.*
78	No replies received.
84	About 53,000 oysters which were scattered have been collected and beds cleaned since last report. 4,030 oysters sold since last report. 8,000 Irish oysters and 5,000 French have been laid down. Moderate fall of spat. Beds in good state, oysters large, fat, and well flavoured. French oysters so far have succeeded; about 100 died shortly after laying down, about half hundred since; they have passed through a very severe winter and are still healthy, but have not fattened or increased in size, although they do not seem so healthy as our native oysters. This is a fattening and breeding bed.
91 / 109	A good deal of labour expended in cleaning the pinnatal parts of vermin and dirt. A good many more than 5,000 native seed oysters laid down, and about 5,000 sold, off outlying portions. Not much fall of spat occurred. Considers bed improving. Floods remain a great destruction to oysters in river.
125	Has laid down 120,000 oysters from Tralee oyster bed, and 58,000 French in prime condition, and has been carefully forming them since, and repairing any breaches in the concrete walls. Sold about 56,000 principally to English dealers, at about £5 per 1,000. Very little spatting if any. Considers bed very flourishing. Calculates about 10 per cent. of the French oysters died in transit or soon after being laid down, the remainder appear to be doing well, and proposes laying down largely this coming season.
154	This license only granted in 1878.
158	This license only granted in 1878.
	County Clare.
23	No replies received.
24	Do.
30	Do.
	County Galway.
10	Nothing done since last report except to keep bed clean and free from trespass. No fall of spat observed. Has not tried French oysters.
15	No replies received.
17	Bed cleaned and oysters scattered since last report. None taken off or sold, but a quantity stolen. No oysters laid down. Spat observed to fall in well sheltered and sunny places, but none on open. Has not laid any French oysters down, as from what he sees on neighbouring beds they do not appear to be doing as anticipated. Remembers beds for 30 years and remarks a falling off in natural production and quantity of spat, nor are the oysters growing so quickly. Attributes this to imperfect knowledge held by breeders of Natural History of oyster.
18	2,000 more French oysters laid down. Only sufficient for home use and presents to friends taken off. Cannot form an estimate as to fall of spat beyond that it appeared a fair one. French oysters have to a certain extent succeeded, but the tide in the Killeries is so strong that, except in places sheltered by a little headland, they are for the most part swept away, but less so than the native oysters; and there is no way of sheltering the shore, which is exposed to all north-west winds.
19	No replies received.
23	Bed cleaned. 5,200 oysters sold. Found a good deal of spat on tiles previous to frost; thinks on an average 24 to each tile. Laid down 24,100 French oysters in April, which did well for some time, but many died during the frost. Will not sell oysters in 1879. Considers bed well stocked with brood.
27	No replies received.
32	Do.
37	Do.
44	Do.
46	Bed regularly cleaned and attended by a trained staff of men. Very few oysters taken off bed within last three years. 650,000 French oysters laid down. Spatting moderate. Beds in a satisfactory state. A considerable mortality in French oysters, considers them rather delicate for the Irish Coast. Had a good fall of spat in artificial pond lately made, and the young oysters are doing well.
81	No replies received.
90	Do.
114	Beds cleaned since last report. 3,000 oysters sold. 20,000 French oysters laid down. Very small fall of spat. French oysters succeeded very well. This winter (1878) numbers died from the frost.
118	Nothing done to bed except removing grass, weeds, and mussels. No oysters sold. About 1,000 French laid down. Considers they are not so good as the native in regard to quality and flavour. Scarcely any spatting. Oysters fast disappearing from locality. Expects all the banks will be covered with mussels; they put in a strong appearance this year after 25 years absence.
136	See replies to License No. 23. No separate account kept.
140	Bed has been watched by two men, but satisfactory work cannot be done till a grant is obtained from Trustees of an Orphanage of a lease of shore opposite their land. About 24 oysters taken off since last season. None put down. No fall of spat.
148	Bed well cared. No oysters taken off. 20,000 French laid down; all appeared safe after transit. Cannot say as to spatting having taken place. Bed in a fair way at present. Hopes to be able to make a better report next season.
149	No replies received.
153	License only granted in 1878.
	County Mayo.
1	Merged into License No. 126, dated 5th July, 1878.
8	Nothing done since last report. No oysters sold; none put down; no spat. The French oysters laid down in former years all died.
11	No replies received.
15	Little or nothing done to beds since last report. No oysters sold and none laid down. Small fall of spat. Beds in good state.
21	No replies received.
23	Nothing except weeding done to bed since last report. 500 oysters sold, none laid down, very little fall of spat. Beds in good state. Fully approves of Colonel Hayes' Report on the French Oyster Fisheries, will give it a trial this season.
31	Nothing done since last report. No oysters taken off bed. Very little, if any, spat. Few oysters on bed; none laid down in 1878. Area comprised within bed being chiefly mud, oysters could not live in it, and what is fit for them is too small to go to any great expense in putting down oysters.
35	Nothing done to bed since last report. No oysters sold; none laid down; no fall of spat.
36	Same reply as No. [illegible]
37	The exceptional severity of the weather impeded, very seriously, operations of any sort on this bed. Now clearing mussels, &c. A considerable quantity of very fine oysters taken off for private use, but none sold. No French oysters laid down this season, but is in treaty for a supply, but the constant frost prevented arrangements being carried out; hopes to make the experiment early in the coming season. Not possible to obtain seed oysters anywhere on these coasts. There appeared to be a fair fall of spat, but a vast quantity is swept away by the force of the tides. Beds appear in a very healthy and flourishing condition, and have proved themselves a success in growing and fattening oysters of excellent quality and flavour. Considers promulgation of information as regards experiments with French brood oysters in this country would be satisfactory.
53	Nothing done to bed since last report, and nothing likely to be done till period for which Clew Bay is closed has elapsed.
54	Bed improved since last report. No oysters sold, about 100 for the use of the Archbishop of Tuam. No French oysters laid down. Laid down a large quantity of Irish oysters and spat.
64	Very little done since last report. No oysters taken off bed. Expects some French oysters, but has not yet received them. A very small fall of spat observed. Oysters planted have grown very large, but from exposed position of bed severe storms and currents affected them very much. Fears bed will never be good for breeding, but will fatten oysters in a short time. The drift sea-weed in stormy weather affects bed very much, lodging on anything placed to catch spat.
69	No replies received.

APPENDIX,

LIST of LICENSES to Plant OYSTER BEDS *in force* on 31st December,

No. of License.	Date of License.	Persons to whom Granted.	Present Owner or Lessee.	Locality of Beds.	Area of Beds. A.	R.	P.	Average area of Beds available. Acres.
71	10th July, 1867,	Townsend Kirkwood,	Townsend Kirkwood,	Salean Harbour,	17	0	0	14
116	25th May, 1872,	William Pike,	William Pike,	Achill Sound,	804	3	29	50
119	3rd July, 1872,	James Rowan,	James Rowan,	Do.,	43	3	0	3
128	1st December, 1873,	Benjamin Whitney,	James M'Donnell,	Blacksod Bay,	41	1	17	
135	4th July, 1874,	Thomas Shaen Carter,	H. T. Shaen Carter,	Trawmore Bay,	862	0	22	200
136	18th August, 1874,	John Kendall,	John Kendall,	Clew Bay,	44	0	37	16
137	4th December, 1874,	Denis Bingham,	Denis Bingham,	Blacksod Bay,	46	1	4	40
140	19th January, 1875,	Michael Moran,	Michael Moran,	Clew Bay,	8	2	2	4
144	24th September, 1875,	Maria Russell,	Maria Russell,	Do.,	4	1	10	4
147	27th December, 1875,	Francis Bourness,	Francis Bourness,	Elly Harbour,	64	2	3	
134	28th December, 1875,	Martin J. Fegan,	Martin J. Fegan,	Clew Bay,	13	3	3	10
142	Do.,	Francis Mulholland,	Francis Mulholland,	Do.,	12	1	22	6
151	27th October, 1876,	William Pike,	William Pike,	Achill Sound,	1,878	0	0	
152	30th October, 1876,	Daniel Conway,	Daniel Conway,	Ballacragher Bay,	2	0	34	
	County Sligo.							
7	27th November, 1863,	Thomas White,	Percy H. Ross,	Ballisodare Bay,	132	1	28	14
49	13th April, 1866,	Sir Robert Gore Booth, bt.,	Sir Henry W. Gore Booth, bt.	Drumcliff Bay,	346	3	0	40
54	1st December, 1866,	Richard J. Verschoyle,	Richard J. Verschoyle,	Ballisodare Bay,	54	0	0	20
69	12th June, 1867,	Sir Robert Gore Booth, bt.,	Owen Rice,	Drumcliff Bay,	67	0	0	10
86	19th March, 1868,	Colonel Edward Cooper,	Colonel Edward Cooper,	Ballisodare Bay,	150	0	0	16
94	14th June, 1869,	John W. Stratford,	John W. Stratford,	Killala Bay,	51	0	0	
98	10th September, 1869,	Henry W. Meredith,	Henry W. Meredith,	Sligo Bay,	28	0	6	3
99	Do.,	Owen Wynne,	Owen Wynne,	Do.,	77	0	0	5
100	Do.,	Do.,	Do.,	Do.,	58	0	2	20
101	12th March, 1870,	R. J. Verschoyle,	R. J. Verschoyle,	Ballisodare Bay,	15	2	0	2
109	22nd April, 1871,	Agnes M. Nicholson,	W. K. Barrett,	Sligo Bay,	53	2	10	25
108	24th April, 1871,	Ed. Park,	Ed. Park,	Milk Haven,	23	0	0	2
107	Do.,	Martin Cunnawn,	Martin Cunnawn,	Do.,	2	2	20	1
106	Do.,	Michael Cunnawn,	Michael Cunnawn,	Do.,	2	1	10	1
121	24th February, 1873,	R. J. Verschoyle,	R. J. Verschoyle,	Ballisodare Bay,	116	0	20	9
127	3rd March, 1873,	Isabella Letitia Eccles,	Isabella Letitia Eccles,	Milk Haven,	28	1	8	9
139	27th January, 1875,	St. Geo. James Martin,	Thomas Gardiner,	Sligo Estuary or Bay,	77	1	33	55
	County Donegal.							
8	22nd September, 1863,	J. O. Woodhouse,	C. O. Woodhouse,	Mulroy Bay,	68	0	26	32
35	31st January, 1864,	William Hart,	The Lessees The Hon. The Irish Society.	Lough Swilly,	780	0	0	200
109	19th July, 1871,	Sir James Stewart, bart.,	Owen Rice,	Do.,	105	2	21	105
113	27th July, 1871,	F. Mansfield,	F. Mansfield,	Do.,	35	1	8	} 10
136	18th October, 1874,	Do.,	Do.,	Do.,	22	0	0	}
148	31st March, 1877,	Alex. J. R. Stewart,	Alex. J. R. Stewart,	Sheephaven,	143	3	18	
150	30th November, 1878,	Jane Moore Doherty,	Jane Moore Doherty,	Lough Foyle,	42	2	30	
	Co. Londonderry.							
149	6th July, 1878,	The Lessees The Hon. The Irish Society.	The Lessees The Hon. The Irish Society.	Lough Foyle,	3,270	3	34	108
	County Down.							
112	8th October, 1872,	Marquess of Downshire,	Marquess of Downshire,	Dundrum Bay,	32	0	2	10
131	24th September, 1874,	Samuel Murland,	Samuel Murland,	Strangford Lough,	18	3	30	15

No. 5—*continued.*

APPENDIX. No. 2.

1878, and Substance of Reports received as to state of Beds—*continued.*

No. of Licence.	Substance of Reports received as to state of Beds.
	County Mayo—continued.
71	Bed carefully preserved. Overplus of oysters collected and placed on bed. No oysters taken off. About 950 native oysters laid down. A reasonable amount of spatting since last report. Bed very promising, would not lay down foreign seed as enough native found on bed. Considers bed will amply repay for outlay.
116	No replies received.
119	Nothing done since last report except oysters occasionally turned. None taken off the beds and none laid down. Much spat did not appear, but could not be seen owing to drifting of sand. Beds in a good state, but drifting of sand does great injury.
275	
136	Bed carefully preserved, no oysters taken off. A fair fall of spat. Bed undoubtedly in good order. No oysters laid down.
138	No replies received.
137	Bed in a very good state. Some native oysters laid down, but cannot state exact quantity.
140	Bed cleaned and raked. No oysters taken off. Could have sold some only for By-law prohibiting the removal of same. Very little spat observed. Beds in a fair state. No French oysters laid down.
144	Bed cleaned since last report. No oysters sold and 6,000 laid down. Good fall of spat. Beds in good state. No French oysters put down.
117	Breeding oysters cared. No oysters taken off bed, none laid down. A large fall of spat this year. Beds very progressive.
180	
141	Bed has been kept clean by dredging since last report. No oysters sold, none put down. Fair show of spat.
151	Oysters redistributed. No oysters sold, a small quantity laid down. Some spat seen.
153	Oysters distributed on bed, which was cleaned of mass since last report. No oysters sold. Some oysters laid down. Fair amount of spat has been seen, but the frost killed a good deal. Beds are improving.
	County Sligo.
7	Bed dredged and cleaned of mussels, &c. About 160,000 French and Irish and 60,000 American oysters taken off the bed, 150,000 French and 100,000 Americans laid down, and 150,000 French and 300,000 Americans were to arrive in a fortnight. No spatting whatever. Bed in good working order, but not sufficiently stocked. French oysters have succeeded very well, very slight loss either in transit or on the beds. The American oyster trade with him likely to become a very large one, part of the bed suiting them admirably. The great disadvantage, however, is not being allowed to send them to England during August, when American oysters bring the highest price.
48	Bed cleaned. 15,000 oysters taken off, about 12,000 oysters laid down. A moderate fall of spat in one part of bed (rocky ground), better than has been for four or five years. French oysters succeeded well, when not injured in transit or not choked by sand; the shell is thin and delicate and easily injured. The running sand which chokes such a number of oysters is principally caused by the digging of slugs adjacent to the bed for baits for fishery purposes. Some of the men state that trawling outside on the bank increases the evil. It is feared this moving sand will eventually destroy the bed, as it did formerly an old Lecanvill Bed.
50	Bed has been cleaned since last report and a quantity of rocks removed and used to form paved beds on which young oysters are placed. Sold about 75,000 oysters since last report, laid down about 22,500 French oysters. There is no sign of spat. Beds are improving. The French oysters purchased previous to this season have done badly, did not grow, and heavy loss by deaths. They were small oysters of 2 years, is now trying a larger and older lot, intending only to hold them for a few months. Has not seen or heard of any spat in Ballisodare Bay since last season. None on his breeding ponds. Spat which was obtained in 1877 is doing well, and came through winter with comparatively little loss.
65	No replies received.
66	Bed picked and kept clean from mussels and dog-wilks. No oysters sold. A few thousand American oysters laid down; intend laying down more. No French oysters put down, found one third of those put down died in transit, or were injured in the shell. Believes they are too young and delicate for transit, the shell being so easily broken; the American ones seem to be stronger and healthier and more likely to spat than the French. No spatting. Bed pretty well stocked.
94	No replies received.
96	Do.
99	Considered it best not to do anything in 1878 except to protect bed. No oysters dredged even for private use.
100	Same as reply to Licence No. 99.
101	See replies to 50 which apply equally to this.
109	Oyster shells and gravel have been put on bed since last report. Between 6,000 and 7,000 oysters sold. 10,000 French oysters and a few thousand Irish laid down. Very little spat. Beds the same since last report. A great number of French oysters died in transit. Those on bed have done well but do not grow to a large size. The bed does not dry at low tide as formerly. Has not been able to gather only to dredge.
106	Scarcely any change in bed since last report. Sold about £5 worth of oysters. French oysters all died. Don't consider last season was good for spatting.
107	Did all he could with bed, put down all the oysters he could but they did no good, owing to being covered by sand and the great frost and snow. No oysters taken off bed. Spat and French oysters all killed by frost. Considers bed good and would be sorry to part with it.
108	Similar replies as to licence, No. 107.
131	See replies to 48, which apply equally to this.
132	Nothing done to bed since last report. About 500 oysters sold. State of bed at present very poor. No oysters laid down. Owing to change in Grange River sand comes in over bed and very little spat can be caught owing to the very strong current.
135	No replies received.
	County Donegal.
6	Beds not interfered with, pending result of experiments with French oysters, on beds in Carlingford Lough—Licences, Nos. 87 and 63.
91	Oysters that were on this bed have all been lifted and taken to Lough Foyle, and licence may be cancelled.
109	No replies received.
116	Quantity of vermin and other matter injurious to oysters removed since last report. 40,000 oysters sold, 2,500 laid down. Little or no spat. Large quantity of oysters killed by frost. No French oysters laid down.
132	Replies to licence, No. 119, refer equally to this bed.
148	A caretaker appointed to preserve bed. A quantity of oysters were stolen. A good natural fall of spat. State of bed as previously. No oysters laid down.
156	Licence only granted in 1878.
	County Londonderry.
149	Beds carefully watched. Some mussels lifted and shipped to Scotland for bait. Only a few oysters lifted, but none sold. A small quantity of spat observed. The oysters laid down appear to be growing and getting into better condition, particularly those brought from Lough Swilly. About 44,000 French oysters purchased in Bordeaux, and laid down in 1877, and it is the intention of the lessees to lay down some more in next March and April, as it is considered those laid down have done very well. They have increased in size very considerably, and also in condition, it is intended to sell some this season. Very few French oysters died in transit or appear to have been lost on the beds.
	County Down.
113	Embankments kept up, large stones taken up and smaller ones put down. No oysters taken off bed. Some young oysters found in enclosure at Ballykinler. Beds in pretty good state except the Murlough Bridge Pond where mud accumulated. No oysters laid down. Intends laying down French oysters, and an additional enclosure has been made between the railway and the street of Dundrum village, and it seems probable that successful spatting might take place at Ballykinler, the difficulty being to retain the fish in the pond, and the sand is a great detriment. The trustees of Lord Downshire have allowed a further small sum towards promoting the object in 1879.
121	Nothing done since last report. The oysters that were laid down died. Next spring intends seeing what can be done.

APPENDIX. Nos. 5 6 7, 8, 9, 10.

APPENDIX,

LIST of LICENSES to Plant OYSTER BEDS *in force* on 31st December,

No. of License	Date of License.	Persons to whom Granted.	Present Owner or Lessee.	Locality of Beds.	Area of Beds.	Average area of Beds available.
	County Louth.				A. R. P.	Acres.
10	1st July, 1854,	Barton Bindon,	Lord Clermont,	Carlingford Lough,	51 2 16	
57	1st December, 1863,	John Obins Woodhouse,	C. O. Woodhouse,	Do.,	56 0 0	50
63	4th June, 1866,	Do.	Do.,	Do.,	66 0 0	
97	16th September, 1869,	Lord Clermont,	Lord Clermont,	Do.,	14 0 0	
111	1st July, 1874,	Arthur Hamill, Q.C.,	Arthur Hamill, Q.C.,	Do.,	144 0 0	
				Total,		

APPENDIX, No. 6.

HERRING FISHERY, 1878.

—	Boats employed, and highest number on any one day				Total Capture.	Average Price.	Value.
	English.	Scotch.	Irish.	Manx.			
					Mease.	£ s. d.	£
Howth, between 24th May and 7th Dec., 1878,	210	215	350	210	68,060	1 3 8	80,694
Arklow, between 9th June and 15th Dec., 1878,	–	–	91	–	6,359	0 16 8	5,285
Kinsale, between 29th April and 21st Dec., 1878,	–	20	22	8	1,372	1 17 5	2,560
Greenore, between 4th June and 27th Nov., 1878,	–	5	45	11	46,754	1 3 8	55,156
Ardglass, between 25th May and 7th Dec., 1878,	40	152	79	37	58,335	1 1 10	63,830
Omeath and Warrenpoint, between 4th June and 19th Oct., 1878,	–	15	50	105	455	1 4 0	546
Kilkeel, between 1st June and 1st Nov., 1878,	200	43	75	–	1,300	1 5 0	1,625
Annalong,	–	–	35	–	9,000	1 0 0	9,000
Courtown,	–	–	35	–	1,968	0 16 0	1,574
					193,603	1 2 9	220,278

APPENDIX No. 7.

MACKEREL FISHERY, 1878.

	Boats employed, and highest number on any one day.	Total Capture.	Average Price.	Amount realized.
		Boxes.	£ s. d.	£
Kinsale,	Irish, 197; Scotch, 90; Manx, 224; English, 38	92,626	1 1 1	97,788

APPENDIX, No. 8.

SUMMARY of the quantity of HERRINGS, MACKEREL, and COD. exported to undermentioned places in England, consigned from Irish Fisheries, from 1st January to 31st December, 1878.

	Herrings. No. of Boxes of 2 cwt. each	Mackerel. No of Boxes of 2 cwt. each.	Cod. No of Boxes of 2 cwt. each.
London,	33,674	28,573	12,670
Nottingham,	3,599	2,842	4,725
Bradford,	17,520	3,777	3,849
Manchester,	8,077	10,665	10,762
Sheffield,	7,554	5,321	1,333
Wolverhampton,	4,121	6,217	3,697
Leeds,	7,961	4,906	3,220
Liverpool,	24,112	13,678	10,670
Birmingham,	11,985	4,221	4,920
Total, 1878,	120,906	80,299	55,546
" 1877,	122,224	83,029	57,839
Decrease,	1,318	2,730	2,293

	£	s.	d.
Computing the Herrings at £2 per box,	241,812	0	0
" the Mackerel, 92,626 boxes, at 21s. 1d. per box,*	97,788	0	0
" the Cod at £3 per box,	166,638	0	0
Total value,	£506,238	0	0

* The only return received was relative to the above-mentioned places, but there were 92,626 boxes captured at Kinsale, the great bulk of which was exported.

No. 5—*continued.*

Appendix. Nos. 5, 6, 7, 8, 9, 10.

1878, and Substance of Reports received as to state of Beds—*continued.*

No. of Licence	Substance of Reports received as to state of Beds.
	County Louth.
10	Nothing done to bed since last report. 44,000 oysters sold in 1878. Did not ascertain if spat had fallen. Beds in a promising state.
57	Several large ponds with sluice gates made. Several thousand oysters taken off for sale or private use. Some spat fell. Bed in fair working order. About 200,000 French oysters laid down, which have succeeded very well, but owing to the severe and continued frost, about 2 per cent. were lost during the winter.
63	For replies see licence, No. 57, which with this form one bed.
97	Nothing done since last report. 4,000 oysters sold, none laid down. Beds reported to be in a healthy state.
111	No replies received.

Appendix, No. 9.

Table showing Loans applied for and advanced under the Irish Reproductive Loan Fund Act during the Year 1878.

County.	Amount available in 1878.	No. of Applications.	No. of Applicants.	Amount of Loans applied for in 1878.	No. of Loans recommended.	No. of Persons to whom Loans recommended.	Amount of Loans recommended in 1878.	No. of Loans actually issued.	Amount of Loans actually issued in 1878.	Loans cancelled or not perfected: No.	Loans cancelled or not perfected: Amount.	Instalments of Loans not taken up: No.	Instalments of Loans not taken up: Amount.	Loans refused for re-application: No.	Loans refused for re-application: Amount.
	£ s. d.			£ s. d.			£ s. d.		£ s. d.		£ s. d.		£ s. d.		£ s. d.
Cork,	850 0 0	53	73	1,872 10 0	17	21	876 0 0	16	859 0 0	1	13 0 0	–	—	–	—
Kerry,	2,450 0 0	131	204	3,832 13 0	100	136	2,407 0 0	91	2,304 0 0	9	103 0 0	–	—	3	72 0 0
Leitrim,	532 0 0	1	1	10 0 0	1	1	10 0 0	–	—	1	10 0 0	–	—	–	—
Limerick,	625 0 0	1	1	6 0 0	–	..	—	–	—	–	—	–	—	–	—
Galway,	1,077 0 0	185	401	5,607 10 0	87	144	1,058 10 0	80	920 10 0	7	80 0 0	7	49 0 0	–	—
Sligo,	449 0 0	31	41	551 12 6	19	37	273 0 0	19	267 0 0	–	—	1	8 0 0	1	24 0 0
Mayo,	693 0 0	88	168	1,873 0 0	61	94	628 0 0	40	553 0 0	2	24 0 0	6	36 0 0	–	—
Clare,	343 0 0	58	55	435 0 0	25	34	282 0 0	24	270 0 0	1	12 0 0	–	—	–	—
Total,	6,741 0 0	558	946	11,808 16 0	300	467	5,588 10 0	270	5,187 10 0	21	208 0 0	14	93 0 0	4	96 0 0

Appendix No. 10.

Table showing Total Amounts advanced on Loan, and the Total Repayments since the passing of Act to 31st December, 1878.

County.	Issued in 1875.	Issued in 1876.	Issued in 1877.	Issued in 1878.	Total Amounts Issued to 31st December, 1878.	Total Repayments to 31st December, 1878.
	£ s. d.	£ s. d.	£ s. d.	£ s. d.	£ s. d.	£ s. d.
Cork,	1,060 0 0	920 0 0	867 0 0	859 0 0	3,706 0 0	2,300 17 10
Kerry,	2,315 0 0	1,218 0 0	114 0 0	2,304 0 0	5,951 0 0	3,196 9 7
Leitrim,	60 0 0	30 0 0	—	—	90 0 0	43 3 0
Limerick,	—	—	—	—	—	—
Galway,	1,162 0 0	1,144 0 0	1,100 0 0	929 10 0	4,335 10 0	2,558 19 7
Sligo,	483 0 0	126 0 0	208 0 0	267 0 0	1,078 0 0	665 10 11
Mayo,	754 0 0	707 0 0	617 0 0	558 0 0	2,636 0 0	1,383 2 2
Clare,	317 0 0	369 0 0	364 0 0	270 0 0	1,320 0 0	608 0 5
Totals,	6,150 0 0	4,512 0 0	3,267 0 0	5,187 10 0	19,106 10 0	10,776 3 6

[Appendix No. 11.

APPENDIX, No. 11.

SCHEDULE of LICENCE DUTIES received by the BOARDS of CONSERVATORS for the Year 1878.

DISTRICT.	Number and Description of Licences sold in 1878.																1878. Amount of Licence Duty.	1878. Poundage on Poor Law Valuation.	1878. Amount received for Fines, Sale of Forfeited Engines, Interest on Bank Account.	1878. Amount of Subscriptions received.	1878. Total Amount received.	1878. Average No. employed.
	1. Salmon Rods.	2. Cross Lines.	3. Snap Nets.	4. Draft Nets.	5. Drift Nets.	6. Trammel Nets for Pollen.	7. Pole Nets.	8. Bag Nets.	9. Fly Nets.	10. Stake Nets.	11. Head Weirs.	12. Box, Crib, &c.	13. Gap, Eye, &c.	14. Sweepers.	15. Coghills.	16. Loop Nets.	£ s. d.	£ s. d.	£ s. d.	£ s. d.	£ s. d.	
1. Dublin,	97	1	-	18	-	-	-	-	-	-	-	-	-	-	-	-	147 0 0	—	4 4 10	—	151 4 10	169
2. Wexford,	87	-	-	64	-	-	-	-	-	-	-	-	-	-	-	-	248 0 0	—	39 4 8	—	284 4 8	407
3. Waterford,	218	14	344	29	00	-	-	-	-	4	-	3	22	-	-	-	1,141 0 0	—	118 1 10	—	1,259 1 10	2,375
4. Lismore,	226	8	20	11	10	-	1	1	-	2	-	2	-	-	-	-	745 10 0	68 0 0	63 0 7	—	876 10 7	873
5. Cork,	282	8	-	78	6	-	-	1	-	1	-	-	-	-	-	-	560 0 0	—	62 0 7	—	622 0 7	735
6¹. Skibbereen,	11	-	-	17	-	-	-	-	-	-	-	-	-	-	-	-	58 0 0	—	2 14 0	—	58 14 0	101
6². Bantry,	12	-	-	12	-	-	-	-	-	-	-	-	-	-	-	-	49 0 0	—	4 13 6	—	53 13 6	85
6³. Kenmare,	22	-	-	7	-	-	-	2	-	-	-	-	-	8	-	-	57 10 0	6 0 0	—	—	63 10 0	98
7. Killarney,	162	4	-	64	-	-	-	-	-	-	-	2	-	-	-	-	302 0 0	27 8 0	78 10 0	39 9 0	447 7 0	493
8. Limerick,	271	42	31	78	177	-	12	-	-	24	1	9	138	-	-	-	2,074 5 0	9 0 0	137 18 0	—	2,414 1 [illegible]	2,046
9. Galway,	147	6	-	12	-	8	-	-	-	-	-	4	21	-	-	-	271 0 0	45 0 0	14 10 0	—	330 10 0	293
10¹. Ballynakill,	57	-	-	17	1	-	8	-	-	-	-	-	-	-	-	-	111 0 0	—	2 0 0	32 10 0	145 10 0	166
10². Bangor,	27	-	-	26	-	-	-	12	-	-	-	-	-	-	-	-	221 0 0	5 0 0	1 8 4	—	231 8 4	221
11. Ballina,	72	-	-	46	38	-	-	6	-	-	-	7	18	-	-	-	461 0 0	—	23 0 6	16 0 0	[illegible]	568
12. Sligo,	14	1	-	10	-	-	-	1	-	-	-	-	4	-	-	-	87 0 0	—	0 18 4	20 0 0	107 18 4	149
13. Ballyshannon,	112	12	-	45	-	-	3	-	-	1	-	4	20	-	-	-	378 0 0	5 0 0	19 5 8	168 2 0	570 8 8	481
14. Letterkenny,	40	-	-	10	12	-	-	8	-	-	-	1	-	-	-	6	179 0 0	14 0 0	5 14 10	—	198 14 10	238
15¹. Londonderry,	77	6	-	51	44	-	2	4	-	5	-	-	-	-	-	-	451 0 0	63 0 0	40 18 8	603 0 0	1,157 18 8	565
15². Coleraine,	91	-	-	133	-	108	-	2	-	-	-	4	-	-	97	-	820 0 0	210 0 0	140 0 0	—	1,170 0 0	1,079
16. Ballycastle,	22	-	-	11	-	-	-	14	-	-	-	-	-	-	-	-	105 0 0	80 0 0	38 11 3	—	237 11 3	144
17¹. Drogheda,	60	8	6	61	-	-	-	-	-	-	-	5	-	-	44	-	303 0 0	—	1 6 8	—	303 8 8	512
17². Dundalk,	47	-	-	25	-	-	-	2	-	-	1	-	87	-	-	-	193 0 0	8 0 0	42 15 6	5 10 0	250 5 6	273
Total,	[illegible]	105	396	797	146	114	26	46	-	44	2	41	257	9	96	6	9,280 0 0	[illegible] 8 0	803 1 2	883 11 0	11,500 0 3	12,106

The estimate of the average number of men employed is made up as follows:—

Salmon Rods, . . 1 man.	Drift Nets, . . 5 men.	Fly Nets, . . . 4 men.	Gap, Eye, &c. . . 2 men.
Cross Lines, . . 2 men.	Trammel Nets, . . 2 do.	Stake Nets, . . . 4 do.	Sweepers, . . . 6 do.
Snap Nets, . . 4 do.	Pole Nets, . . . 3 do.	Head weirs, . . . 1 man.	Coghills, . . . 1 man.
Draft Nets, . . 6 do.	Bag Nets, . . . 4 do.	Box, crib, &c. (every 3) 1 man.	Loop or Frame Nets, 1 do.

APPENDIX, No. 12.

TABLE showing the Total Amount received in the various Fishery Districts from the sale of Licences between the years 1863 and 1878, inclusive.

	Amount received for Licence Duty. £ s. d.		Amount received for Licence Duty. £ s. d.		Amount received for Licence Duty. £ s. d.
1863 . . .	4,892 7 6	1869 . . .	6,700 6 4	1874 . . .	9,418 9 0
1864 . . .	6,841 5 0	1870 . . .	7,511 13 4	1875 . . .	8,417 1 5
1865 . . .	6,722 16 8	1871 . . .	8,865 15 9	1876 . . .	9,878 5 10
1866 . . .	7,096 6 8	1872 . . .	8,968 1 0	1877 . . .	9,790 15 0
1867 . . .	7,317 0 8	1873 . . .	9,040 14 0	1878 . . .	9,785 19 0
1868 . . .	7,833 19 5				

Increase in Licence Duty since 1863, £4,843 [illegible]s. [illegible]d.

APPENDIX, No. 13.

SCHEDULE of LICENSE DUTIES payable in each District on Engines used for Fishing for Salmon, January, 1879.

District	1. [illegible]	2. [illegible]	3. [illegible]	4. [illegible]	5. [illegible]	6. [illegible]	7. [illegible]	8. [illegible]	9. [illegible]	10. [illegible]	11. [illegible]	12. [illegible]	13. [illegible]	14. [illegible]	15. [illegible]	16. [illegible]
	£ s. d.	£ s. d.	£ s. d.	£ s. d.	£ s. d.	£ s. d.	£ s. d.	£ s. d.	£ s. d.	£ s. d.	£ s. d.	£ s. d.	£ s. d.	£ s. d.	£ s. d.	£ s. d.
1. Dublin	[illegible]	[illegible]	[illegible]	[illegible]	[illegible]	[illegible]	[illegible]						[illegible]	—	—	—
2. Wexford	[illegible]	[illegible]	[illegible]	[illegible]	[illegible]	[illegible]	[illegible]						[illegible]	—	—	—
3. Waterford	[illegible]	[illegible]	[illegible]	[illegible]	[illegible]	[illegible]	[illegible]						[illegible]	—	—	—
4. Lismore	[illegible]	[illegible]	[illegible]	[illegible]	[illegible]	[illegible]	[illegible]						[illegible]	—	—	—
5. Cork	[illegible]	[illegible]	[illegible]	[illegible]	[illegible]	[illegible]	[illegible]						[illegible]	—	—	—
6. [illegible]	[illegible]	[illegible]	[illegible]	[illegible]	[illegible]	[illegible]	[illegible]						[illegible]	—	—	—
7. Bantry	[illegible]	[illegible]	[illegible]	[illegible]	[illegible]	[illegible]	[illegible]						[illegible]	—	—	—
8. Kenmare	[illegible]	[illegible]	[illegible]	[illegible]	[illegible]	[illegible]	[illegible]						[illegible]	[illegible]	[illegible]	—
9. Killarney	[illegible]	[illegible]	[illegible]	[illegible]	[illegible]	[illegible]	[illegible]						[illegible]	—	—	—
10. Limerick	[illegible]	[illegible]	[illegible]	[illegible]	[illegible]	[illegible]	[illegible]						[illegible]	—	—	—
11. Galway	[illegible]	[illegible]	[illegible]	[illegible]	[illegible]	[illegible]	[illegible]						[illegible]	—	—	—
12. [illegible]	[illegible]	[illegible]	[illegible]	[illegible]	[illegible]	[illegible]	[illegible]	[illegible]	[illegible]	[illegible]	[illegible]	[illegible]	[illegible]	—	—	—
13. Bangor	[illegible]	[illegible]	[illegible]	[illegible]	[illegible]	[illegible]	[illegible]						[illegible]	—	—	—
14. Ballina	[illegible]	[illegible]	[illegible]	[illegible]	[illegible]	[illegible]	[illegible]						[illegible]	—	—	—
15. Sligo	[illegible]	[illegible]	[illegible]	[illegible]	[illegible]	[illegible]	[illegible]						[illegible]	—	—	—
16. Ballyshannon	[illegible]	[illegible]	[illegible]	[illegible]	[illegible]	[illegible]	[illegible]						[illegible]	—	[illegible]	—
17. Letterkenny	[illegible]	[illegible]	[illegible]	[illegible]	[illegible]	[illegible]	[illegible]						[illegible]	—	[illegible]	[illegible]
18. Londonderry	[illegible]	[illegible]	[illegible]	[illegible]	[illegible]	[illegible]	[illegible]						[illegible]	—	—	—
19. Coleraine	[illegible]	[illegible]	[illegible]	[illegible]	[illegible]	[illegible]	[illegible]						[illegible]	—	[illegible]	—
20. [illegible]	[illegible]	[illegible]	[illegible]	[illegible]	[illegible]	[illegible]	[illegible]						[illegible]	—	—	—
21. [illegible]	[illegible]	[illegible]	[illegible]	[illegible]	[illegible]	[illegible]	[illegible]						[illegible]	—	[illegible]	[illegible]
22. [illegible]	[illegible]	[illegible]	[illegible]	[illegible]	[illegible]	[illegible]	[illegible]						[illegible]	—	[illegible]	—

Appendix, No. 14.

Abstract of By-Laws, Orders, &c.

Appendix, No. 14.

Abstract of By-Laws, Orders, &c., in force on 1st January, 1879, relating to the Salmon Fisheries of Ireland.

Place affected by By-Law, and Date thereof.	Nature of By-Law.
	SALMON AND TROUT.
	Dublin District.
River Liffey, (19th Jan., 1863.)	Prohibiting the catching, or attempting to catch, Salmon with any Net of greater length than 350 yards, in that part of the River Liffey which is situated between the Weir known as the Island Bridge Weir and a line drawn due North from Poolbeg Lighthouse.
Between Dalkey Island and Wicklow Head. (15th Oct., 1874.)	Permitting use of Nets with Meshes of one inch from knot to knot for capture of Salmon or Trout between Dalkey Island and Wicklow Head.
	Wexford District.
River Slaney, (25th March, 1854, and 24th March, 1862.)	Prohibiting, during the Close Season for Salmon, the use of Nets of any kind whatsoever, between Ferrycarrig Bridge and the Town of Enniscorthy.
	Prohibiting, during the Open Season for Salmon, the use of Nets with meshes of less size than one and three-quarter inches from knot to knot, between Ferrycarrig Bridge and the Town of Enniscorthy.
Derry Water and River Derry. (28th Oct., 1870.)	Permitting use of Nets for the capture of Fish, having Meshes of one inch from knot to knot (to be measured along the side of the square, or four inches, to be measured all round each such Mesh, such measurements being taken in the clear when the Net is wet), in the rivers and streams following, that is to say, in the Derry Water, from its source near Kilbavney to Annacurragh Bridge, with the streams flowing into same from Moyne Church through Ballinglen, and the Tomnaskela River; and in the Greenisland, Shillelagh and Derry River, from the bounds of the County Carlow, flowing past Tinahely by Shillelagh to the bounds of the County Wexford, with the small streams flowing into that portion of the said river, all said rivers and streams being in the County Wicklow, for and during the months of May, June, July, and August, in each year.
Potter River, (28th Oct., 1870.)	Permitting use of Nets for the capture of Fish with Meshes of one inch from knot to knot (to be measured along the side of the square, or four inches to be measured all round each such Mesh, such measurements being taken in the clear, when the Net is wet), in the tidal portion of the Potter River, situated below [illegible] Bridge in the County of Wicklow.
Owenavorragh River, (15th Feb., 1875.)	Permitting use of nets with meshes of one inch from knot to knot for capture of salmon or trout.
	Waterford District.
Bessborough Demesne, Co. Kilkenny (18th May, 1868.)	Permitting the use of Nets for the capture of Fish with Meshes of one inch from knot to knot (to be measured along the side of the square, or four inches to be measured all round each such Mesh, such measurements being taken in the clear, when the Net is wet,) within the Waters in, and Rivers running through the Demesne of Bessborough, in the County of Kilkenny: Provided that no Net having a less Mesh than one inch and three-quarters from knot to knot, shall be used in the said Rivers during the Months of April, May, and June.
Corrach River, (7th July, 1870.)	Permitting use of Nets with Meshes of one inch from knot to knot (to be measured along the side of the square, or four inches to be measured all round each Mesh, such measurements being taken in the clear when the Net is wet).
River Suir, (17th Aug., 1875.)	Prohibiting use of all Engines (save single Rods and Lines) for capture of Fish, between the Bridges at Suir Island and a line drawn due south across the River, and intersecting said Island at Clonmel.
River Suir, Nore, and Barrow, conjoined, (14th March, 1878.)	Prohibiting to use for the capture of Salmon or Trout any Draft Net in the Tidal portions of the River Suir, Nore, and Barrow, above a line drawn across said River from Cheekpoint, County Waterford on the West, in an Easterly direction to Campile Pill, in the County Wexford.
	Lismore District.
Between Helvick Head and Ballycotton, River Blackwater, &c. (6th Nov., 1874.)	Repealing By-law of 2nd November, 1870, regulating Drift Net Fishing, and in lieu thereof providing as follows:—
	First.—That no Drift Nets of greater length than 300 yards shall be used for the capture of Salmon and Trout in the Rivers or Estuaries flowing into the sea between Helvick Head and Ballycotton, or in the sea between those points.
	Second.—That no two or more Drift Nets when fishing shall be attached together in any way.
	Third.—That Drift Nets shall not be used at a less distance from each other than fifty yards in that portion of the River Blackwater situated within one mile of the mouth of the River as at present defined, each Drift Net shot and drifting to be kept at a distance of not less than fifty yards from the one preceding it on the tide and already drifting.
River Blackwater. (14th March, 1878.)	Prohibiting to use for the capture of Salmon or Trout any Drift Net in the Tidal portion of the River Blackwater, or its Tributaries, above or to the Northward of a line drawn across said River from the Townland Boundary between the Townlands of [illegible] and Newport East on the West, to the Townland Boundary between the Townlands of Coolbeggan and Ballynaclash on the East, all in the County of Waterford.
	Cork District.
Tidal Waters, (11th Sept., 1868.)	Prohibiting the catching or attempting to catch Salmon or Trout in any Tidal Water in the Cork District with a Spear, Lyster, Otter, Strokehaul, Dree Draw, or Gaff, except when the latter instrument may be used solely as auxiliary to angling with Rod and Line, or for the purpose of removing Fish from any legal Weir or Box by the Owner or Occupier thereof.
	Prohibiting the snatching or attempting to snatch Salmon or Trout in any Tidal or Fresh Water in the Cork District with any kind of Fish-hook, covered in part or in whole with any matter or thing, or uncovered.
River Lee, Co. of the City of Cork. (7th January, 1863.)	Prohibiting, during the Close Season for Salmon the use of Draft Nets, or any other Net or Nets used as a Draft Net, having a foot-rope and leads or weights affixed thereto, within the following limits, viz.:—in that part of the River Lee, situate between Patrick's Bridge, in the City of Cork, and a line drawn across the said River Lee, from Blackrock Castle, on the south, to the Western extremity of the Townland of Dunkettle, on the North.
River Lee, (21st April, 1871.)	Prohibiting use of all Nets except Landing-Nets, as auxiliary to rods and lines in part of South Channel between George IV. Bridge and Friar's Walk.
River Lee, (31st March, 1876.)	Prohibiting the catching or attempting to catch Fish of any kind in that part of the River Lee situated between the Cork Waterworks Weir and St. Vincent's Bridge in the North Channel, and Clarke's Bridge in the South Channel, and in the mill races and inlets from such channels with a Spear, Lyster, Otter, Strokehaul, Dree-draw or Gaff, except when the latter instrument may be used solely as auxiliary to angling with Rod and Line, or for the purpose of removing Fish from any legal Weir or Box by the owner or occupier thereof.
River Lee & Rivers running into Cork Harbour. (16th Feb., 1877.)	Prohibiting the use of Drift Nets for Salmon or Trout in any Tidal Waters inside of to north of a line from Lighthouse at Roche's Point to mainland on the West.
Ditto, (28th Sept., 1878.)	Prohibiting to use any Net for the capture of Salmon or Trout in any Tidal Water, inside or to North of a line from Lighthouse at Roche's Point to Mainland on the West, having Meshes of greater dimensions than two and one-half inches from knot to knot, to be measured along the side of the square, or ten inches to be measured all round each such Mesh, such measurements being taken in the clear when the Net is wet.
River Lee, (29th Sept., 1877.)	Prohibiting having Nets for capture of Salmon or Trout on board any Boat, Cot, or Curragh in that part of River seaward of a line drawn due south from the Western end of Myrtle

APPENDIX, No. 14—*continued.*

APPENDIX, No. 14. Abstract of By-Law, Orders, &c.

ABSTRACT of BY-LAWS, ORDERS, &c., in force on 1st January, 1879, relating to the SALMON FISHERIES of IRELAND.

Place affected by By-Law, and Date thereof	Nature of By-Law.
	Cork District—*continued.*
River Lee—*continued.*	Hill-terrace on the north, near a place known as the Brick Fields, to the opposite shore, or in the tidal part of any river flowing into River Lee, between 8 o'clock on Saturday morning and 6 o'clock on Monday morning; or in that part of said River between the line mentioned above and the point of the Custom House in the City of Cork between 8 o'clock on Saturday morning and half-past 5 o'clock on Monday morning, or in the North Channel of said River between Northgate Bridge and Wellington Bridge, or in the South Channels between the slip at Dunbar Bridge opposite Keyser's Hill, leading to Crosse's Green and St. Fin Barr's Quay, and the Bridge where the Western Road crosses South Channel, between 8 o'clock on Saturday morning and 6 o'clock on Monday morning.
Argideen River, (24th Feb., 1869.)	Prohibiting the use of Nets of any kind whatsoever in the tidal part of the river known as the Argideen River, in the County of Cork, situated between the junction of the Owenkeagh or Blind River with the said Argideen River and the Bridge of Timoleague, all in the Barony of the East Division of East Carbery, and County of Cork.
Argideen River, (16th Feb., 1877.)	Prohibiting the use of Drift Nets for Salmon or Trout in Tidal Waters inside a line from Land Point in an easterly direction to the opposite shore.
Bandon River, (16th Dec., 1874.)	Prohibiting for five years from the 1st January, 1875, the use of all Nets (except Landing Nets as auxiliary to angling with Rod and Line) for the capture of Salmon or Trout in any part of said River or its Tributaries, above a line drawn across the said River at right angles with the River's course from the Stream on the east side of said River, dividing the Townlands of Coolmorreen and Skeamague to the Stream on the opposite shore dividing the Townlands of Drumkeen and Knockroe.
Bandon River, (16th Feb., 1877.)	Prohibiting the use of Drift Nets for Salmon or Trout in Tidal Waters inside a line from Blackeen Point in an easterly direction to Preghane Point.
	Skibbereen District.
River Ilen, (22nd Feb., 1874.)	Permitting use of Nets with Meshes of one and a quarter inches from knot to knot for capture of Salmon or Trout.
	Bantry District.
Tidal Waters, (7th March, 1870.)	Permitting use of Nets of a Mesh of one and a quarter inches from knot to knot (to be measured along the side of the square, or five inches to be measured all round each such Mesh, such measurements being taken in the clear when the Net is wet), in the tidal waters of the Bantry District, which comprises the whole of the sea along the coast between Mizen Head in the County Cork and Crow Head in the same County, and around any Islands or Rocks situate off same, with the whole of the Tideways along said Coast and Rivers, and the whole of the tidal portions of the several Rivers and their Tributaries flowing into said Coast.
Snave or Coomhola, Mealagh, or Dunamark, Owvane, and Carrigboy Rivers. (21st June, 1871.)	Prohibiting use of all Nets, save Landing Nets, as auxiliary to rods and lines in fresh-water portions of said Rivers.
	Killarney District.
Castlemaine Estuary (27th Oct., 1858.)	Prohibiting, during the Salmon Close Season, the use of Draft Nets having a foot-rope and leads or weights affixed thereto, in the Estuary of Castlemaine inside the Bar of Inch.
Tidal Waters, (8th Feb., 1865.)	Prohibiting the catching, or attempting to catch Salmon in any tidal water with a Spear, Lyster, Otter, Strokehaul, Dree-Draw, or Gaff, except when the latter instrument may be used solely as auxiliary to angling with rod and line, or for the purpose of removing fish from any legal Weir or Box by the owner or occupier thereof.
	Killarney District—*continued.*
Currane or Waterville River—Waterville Weir (7th March, 1870.)	Permitting the space between the Bars or Rails of the Inscales and of the Heck or upstream side of the Boxes or Cribs at the Waterville Weir to be one and a quarter inches apart.
Waterville River, (16th Feb., 1871.)	Prohibiting use of Nets between Waterville Weir and mouth of River as defined, between twelve o'clock noon on Friday and six o'clock on Saturday morning, and between six o'clock Monday morning and twelve o'clock noon same day in each week during Open Season.
	Limerick District.
River Shannon, Island Point. (8th Feb., 1856.)	Prohibiting Net Fishing in that part of the River Shannon between Wellesley Bridge and the Railway Bridge, between 1st June and 12th February.
River Shannon, (22nd Nov., 1862.)	Prohibiting Draft Nets for the capture of Fish of any kind, of a mesh less than one and three-quarter inches from knot to knot, to be measured along the side of the square, or seven inches to be measured all round each such mesh, such measurements being taken in the clear when the Net is wet, in the tidal parts of the River Shannon, or in the tidal parts of any of the Rivers flowing into the said River Shannon.
River Shannon, (8th May, 1866.)	Prohibiting the Fishing for Salmon or Trout by any means whatsoever, within a space of Twenty Yards from the Weir Wall of Tarmonbarry, on the River Shannon.
Rivers Shannon and Maigue (5th June, 1867.)	Prohibiting the Snatching of Fish in that part of River Shannon between Portumna Bridge and Shannon Bridge, and also in River Maigue.
River Shannon, (1st March, 1872.)	Prohibiting having Nets for capture of Salmon or Trout on board any Cot or Curragh between mouth of Shannon and Wellesley Bridge, in the city of Limerick, or in tidal parts of any rivers flowing into the said River Shannon between said points between the hours of Nine o'clock on Saturday morning and Three o'clock on Monday morning; or between Wellesley Bridge and the Navigation Weir at Killaloe in the County of Clare, between Eight o'clock on Saturday morning and Four o'clock on Monday morning.
Rivers Shannon, Maigue, and Askeaton, and Clonderlaw Bay. (18th Nov., 1874.)	Regulating the use of Drift Nets as follows:— First.—That no Drift Nets of greater length than 100 yards shall be used for the capture of Salmon or Trout in any part of the River Shannon between Limerick and a line drawn across the River below Askeaton, from Aughinish Point, in the County of Limerick, to Kildysart, in the County of Clare. Second.—That no Drift Nets of greater length than 200 yards shall be used for the capture of Salmon or Trout in any other Tidal Waters of the River Shannon, or in Clonderlaw Bay. Third.—That no two or more Drift Nets shall be attached together in any way or be allowed to drift within 150 yards of each other in the River Shannon, or in Clonderlaw Bay. Fourth.—That no Drift Nets below or seaward of a line drawn across the River Shannon, from Aughinish Point, in the County of Limerick, to Kildysart, in the County of Clare, shall be used within the line of low water mark of ordinary Spring Tides. Fifth.—That no Drift Nets shall be used in Clonderlaw Bay above a line drawn from Knock to Lackanalahee, in the County of Clare. Sixth.—That no Drift Nets shall be used in the Rivers Maigue or Askeaton.
River Deel, (8th June, 1877).	Prohibiting the use of all Nets (except Landing Nets as auxiliary to angling with rod and line) for the capture of Salmon or Trout, in that part of River situate between Broken Bridge and the mouth of River as defined.
Lough Derg, (19th June, 1877.)	Permitting the use of Nets not exceeding 12 yards in length, with Meshes of one inch from knot to knot for the capture of fish other than Salmon or Trout.
Ditto, (19th June, 1877.)	Prohibiting the use of Nets (except Landing Nets as auxiliary to angling with rod and line) for the capture of Fish other than Eels, between 8 o'clock in the evening and 6 o'clock in the morning.

Appendix, No. 14—*continued*.

Abstract of By-Laws, Orders, &c., in force on 1st January, 1879, relating to the Salmon Fisheries of Ireland.

Place affected by By-Law, and Date thereof.	Nature of By-Law.
	Limerick District—*continued*.
River Shannon, . (23rd June, 1877.)	Repealing the first clause of By-law dated 22nd November, 1862, and in lieu thereof prohibiting between the 1st day of August, or such other day as at time may be the first day of the Close Season in which no Fish of the Salmon or Trout kind shall be killed, destroyed, or taken by any person or by any means whatsoever (save by single rod and line only), and the 1st day of November in each year, the use of Draft Nets or any other Net or Nets used as a Draft Net, having a foot rope and leads or weights affixed thereto, in that part of the River Shannon extending between the Fishing Weir known as the Lax Weir and a line drawn due North and South across the said River Shannon at the Western extremity of Graigue Island.
Lough Ree, River Shannon. (27th August, 1858.)	Permitting the use of Nets in Lough Ree, having a mesh of five inches in the round, measured when the Net is wet.
River Fergus, . (20th June, 1865.)	Prohibiting the Fishing for Salmon or Trout by any means whatsoever, within a space of Twenty Yards from the Weir Wall of Ennis, on the River Fergus.
River Fergus, . (16th Dec., 1870.)	Prohibiting the use of Drift Nets in the Tidal parts of River Fergus, County Clare.
River Maigue, . (17th Oct., 1864.)	Prohibiting the use of Draft Nets between Ferry Dunwbridge and the old Bridge of Adare.
Maigue River, . (1st March, 1871.)	Prohibiting use of all Nets, except Landing-Nets as auxiliary to rod and line, above Railway-bridge below Adare.
	Galway District.
Galway River, Lough Corrib, &c. (24th July, 1848.)	Prohibiting the use of the Instrument, commonly called Stokehaul or Snatch, or any other such instrument, in River Galway, Loughs Corrib or Mask, or their Tributaries.
Whole District, . (11th Sept., 1866.)	Prohibiting the snatching or attempt to snatch Salmon in any Tidal or Fresh Water in the Galway District with any kind of Fish-hook, covered in part or in whole with any matter or thing, or uncovered.
Clare and Clare-Galway or Turloughmore Rivers, Co. Galway. (22nd Dec., 1862.)	Prohibiting the use of Nets of any kind whatsoever in any part of the Rivers known as the Clare and the Clare-Galway or Turloughmore Rivers, in the County of Galway, above the junction of the said Rivers with Lough Corrib, in the County of Galway.
	Bangor District.
Owenmore River, Co. Mayo. (5th May, 1866.)	Prohibiting the removal of gravel or sand from any part of the bed of the Owenmore River, in the County of Mayo, where the spawning of Salmon or Trout may take place.
Owenduff or Ballycroy, Owenmore and Munhin Rivers. (11th Sept., 1866.)	Permitting the use of Nets with Meshes of one and a-half inches from knot to knot (to be measured along the side of the square, or six inches to be measured all round each such Mesh, such measurements being taken in the clear, when the Net is wet,) within so much of the said Rivers Owenduff or Ballycroy, Owenmore and Munhin, as lies above the mouth as defined, during so much of the Months of June, July, and August, as do now or at any time may form part of the Open Season for the capture of Salmon or Trout, with Nets, in the said Rivers.
	Ballina District.
Whole District, . (21st May, 1870.)	Permitting use of Nets with Meshes of one and a quarter inches from knot to knot (to be measured along the side of the square, or five inches to be measured all round each such Mesh, such measurements being taken in the clear, when the Net is wet).
Moy River and Tributaries. (11th Feb., 1871.)	Prohibiting angling for Trout during April and May in each year—Loughs Conn and Cullen excepted.
	Sligo District.
Sligo River, . (1st March, 1870.)	Prohibiting the snatching or attempting to snatch Salmon in Sligo River, with any kind of Fish-hook covered in part or in whole, or uncovered.
Lough Deen, . (24th March, 1871.)	Permitting use of Nets with meshes of half an inch from knot to knot, for capture of Fish.
	Ballyshannon District.
Erne River, . . (18th Feb., 1871.)	Permitting use of Nets with meshes of one inch from knot to knot in tideway of River Erne.
Ditto, . . (1st June, 1872.)	Prohibiting the capture of Fish of any description with the instrument commonly called and known by the name of the Spoonbait, or any other instrument of the like nature or device during the months of January, February, and March in each year, in that part of the River Erne situated between the Falls of Belleek and a line drawn due south across the River, from the grounds of Castlecaldwell demesne, by the Eastern point of the Muckinish, or White Island, to the opposite Bank, all in the County of Fermanagh.
Lower Lough Erne, (20th June, 1874.)	Permitting use of nets with meshes of one inch from knot to knot for capture of fish by persons having right to use nets in said lough, between Enniskillen and Belleek, between 1st May and first day of close season in each year.
Eany Water, or Inver River. (25th June, 1872.)	Permitting use of Nets for the capture of Fish with Meshes of one inch from knot to knot (to be measured along the side of the square, or four inches to be measured all round each such Mesh, such measurements being taken in the clear when the Net is wet), within so much of the River Eany Water, or Inver, in the County of Donegal, as lies above the mouth of said river as defined.
	Letterkenny District.
Crana or Buncrana River. (5th Nov., 1877.)	Permitting the use of nets for the capture of Salmon or Trout with Meshes of one inch from knot to knot in the Crana or Buncrana River, and within one mile seawards and coastwards thereof.
	Londonderry District.
River Foyle, . (28th Feb., 1871.)	Permitting the use of Nets with meshes of one inch from knot to knot in Lough Foyle and tidal parts of River.
Baronscourt Lakes and Streams. (22nd April, 1871.)	Permitting the use of Nets for the capture of fish, other than Salmon and Trout, with meshes of half an inch from knot to knot.
Tidal Waters, . (5th June, 1878.)	Prohibiting having nets for capture of Salmon or Trout in or on board any boat, cot, or curragh in the Tidal Waters of said district, which comprises the whole of the sea along the coast between Malin Head, in the County of Donegal, and the townland boundary between the townlands of Drumagully and Downhill, in the County of Londonderry, with the whole of the tideway along said coast and rivers, and the whole of the tidal portion of the several rivers and their tributaries flowing into said coast between said points, at any time between the hours of twelve of the clock at noon on Saturday and four of the clock on Monday morning.
	Coleraine District.
Lough Neagh, . (16th Feb., 1867.)	Prohibiting the use of Draft Nets for the capture of Pollen.
Lough Neagh, . (20th Feb., 1871.)	Permitting Pollen to be taken by Trammel or Set Nets composed of Thread or Yarn of a fine texture, not less than ten hanks to the pound weight, doubled and twisted with a mesh of not less than one inch from knot to knot, from the 1st of February to the 31st October.
Whole District, . (17th Oct., 1870.)	Prohibiting snatching or attempting to snatch Salmon in any of the tidal or fresh waters of District.
	Ballycastle District.
Bush River, . . (25th Feb., 1870.)	Repealing Definition of Bush River Estuary as fixed by the late Special Commissioners on 8th February, 1864.
	Dundalk District.
Between Clogher Head and Bellaghan Point (30th April, 1872)	Prohibiting to catch or attempting to catch Salmon or Trout with any Net of greater length than 800 Yards in that part of the Sea Coast situated between Clogher Head and Bellaghan Point, in the County of Louth.
Tidal Waters, . (30th June, 1873.)	Prohibiting the catching or attempting to catch Salmon in any Tidal water of District between Dunany Point and Soldier's Point, in the County Louth, with a Spear, Lyster, Otter, Strokehaul, Draw-drew, or Gaff, except when the latter may be used solely as auxiliary to angling with Rod and Line, or for removing fish from any legal Weir or Box by the Owner or Occupier thereof.

APPENDIX, No. 15.

APPENDIX No. 15.

RIVERS, the Mouths of which have been defined in 1878, and to 31st March, 1879, making, with those enumerated in previous Reports, 148 in number.

District.	Name of River.	District.	Name of River.
Limerick, ...	Annagh.	Coleraine, ...	Main.
Do., ...	Annageeragh.	Do., ...	Blackwater.
Kenmare, ...	Tahilla.	Do., ...	Sixmilewater.
Coleraine, ...	Moyola.	Do., ...	Bann (Upper).
Do., ...	Ballinderry.		

APPENDIX, No. 16.

APPENDIX, No. 16.

RIVERS, the TIDAL and FRESH WATER BOUNDARIES of which have been defined to 31st March, 1879.

River.	Boundary.	Date	
Adrigole, . .	Adrigole Bridge, ...	10th June,	1871.
Annagh, . .	Beelaninga Bridge, between the townlands of Dough and Annagh, ...	27th November,	1878.
Annageeragh, .	The barrier of stones at seaward side of Lough Donnell, between the townlands of Clogh-aunsodohy and Cloonmagarmaun.	27th November,	1878.
Bandon, . .	The Bridge at Inneshannon, known as the Inneshannon Bridge, ...	19th January,	1868.
Bann, . . .	The Down Stream end of Fishing Weir, known as the Cutts, ...	28th November,	1875.
Barrow, . .	The lowest Weir or Dam used for navigation purposes, near St. Mullins, in county Carlow, . .	16th March,	1864.
Blackwater, . .	A straight line drawn due north across river at townland boundary between townlands of Ballynafligan Glebe and Ballynaweat.	15th March,	1872.
Boyne, . . .	Eastern Point of Grove Island at Oldbridge, ...	8th April,	1865.
Bride, . . .	Tallow Bridge Quay, ...	26th January,	1874.
Carragh, . .	The Carragh Bridge, being the bridge immediately seaward of the Salmon Weir, ...	10th January,	1868.
Carrigloy, . .	Carrigloy Bridge, ...	10th June,	1871.
Dee, . . .	Willistown Weir, ...	20th May,	1872.
Deel or Askeaton, .	Askeaton Bridge, ...	29th November,	1870.
Eske, . . .	Foot Bridge above Donegal Bridge, ...	17th July,	1868.
Fane, . . .	The Railway Bridge across said River, ...	16th May,	1871.
Feale, . . .	The Road leading through Killacrim from the Road leading from Listowel to Ennismore by a line drawn in continuation of said Killacrim Road across River.	4th October,	1875.
Fergus, . . .	The Bridge commonly known as the New Bridge, immediately below the Club House, at Ennis,	9th April,	1864.
Flesk, . . .	A straight line drawn in a westerly direction across river at townland boundary between townlands of Quarter and Rewley.	15th March,	1879.
Galey or Geale, .	The Stream called and known by the name of the Gerah-Gloss, between the townlands of Gortacrossane and Bouanamodane.	4th October,	1875.
Glengarriffe, . .	Greenwell's Bridge, ...	10th June,	1871.
Glenshelane, . .	The bridge across river known as the Little Bridge near Cappoquin, ...	15th March,	1879.
Glyde, . . .	Lynn's Weir, ...	28th May,	1872.
Goish, . . .	A straight line drawn in a north easterly direction across river from a point on townland of Dromore, at the road leading to Villierstown, to a point on the townland of Coolahest.	15th March,	1879.
Greagagh, . .	A straight line drawn in a north westerly direction across river at the townland boundary between the townlands of Raheen and Ballyheeny.	15th March,	1879.
Inch, . . .	Adare Bridge, ...	1st February,	1868.
Laune, . . .	The shallow at the head of the Pool, commonly called the Cat Pool, ...	29th July,	1863.
Lee, . . .	The Weir or Dam at the Water Works of Cork, known as the Water Works Weir, . .	12th August,	1864.
Lickey, . . .	The bridge across river known as the Ballyheeny Bridge, ...	15th March,	1879.
Liffey, . . .	The Weir or Dam on said river known as the Island Bridge Weir, ...	12th August,	1864.
Maigue, . . .	The Bridge across river immediately outside and seaward of the Adare Demesne, . . .	12th August,	1864.
Maine, . . .	A straight line drawn across river at right angles with its course at the boundary between the townlands of Cooleleave and Ballyfinnane.	29th July,	1863.
Mealagh or Dunnamark.	Wooden Bridge at Dunnamark Mill, ...	10th June,	1871.
Moy, . . .	The foot of the falls immediately below the Weirs at Ballina, ...	29th July,	1865.
Nore, . . .	The Inistiogue Bridge, ...	16th March,	1864.
Owvane or Bally-lickey.	The Ballylickey Bridge on the High Road, ...	10th June	1871.
Shannon, . .	The Weir or Dam known as the Corbally Mill Weir, ...	9th April,	1864.
Shimna, . .	The Castle Bridge near Newcastle, ...	26th August,	1869.
Slaney, . . .	Enniscorthy Bridge, ...	1st February,	1866.
Sligo or Garvogue,	The Mill Dam above Victoria Bridge, in town of Sligo, ...	15th February,	1871.
Snave or Coomhola,	Snave Bridge, ...	10th June,	1871.
Suir, . . .	A line drawn across river at and opposite to the most up-stream part of the Coolnamuck Weir,	16th March,	1864.
Tahilla, . .	The mouth of river as defined 21st November, 1878, by a straight line drawn in a north easterly direction across said river from a point on townland of Tahilla to a point on townland of Derreenanamucklagh	5th February,	1879.
Trawig, . .	The bridge known as the Two Mile Bridge, ...	15th March,	1872.

APPENDIX,

TABLE showing the CLOSE SEASONS for SALMON and TROUT in

No. and Name of District.	Boundary of District.	Tidal.
1. Dublin,	Skerries to Wicklow.	From Howth to Dalkey Island, between 15th August and 1st February. For remainder of District, between 15th September and 2nd March.
2. Wexford,	Wicklow to Kiln Bay, East of Bannow Bay.	Between 15th September and 30th April.
3. Waterford,	Kiln Bay to Helvick Head.	" 15th August and 1st February.
4. Lismore,	Helvick Head to Ballycotton.	" 31st August and 16th February.
5. Cork,	Ballycotton Head to Galley Head.	" 15th August and the 15th of Feb., save in Bandon and Argideen Rivers; between 15th August and 1st March for Bandon, and between 31st August and 1st March for Argideen.
6a. Skibbereen,	Galley Head to Mizen Head.	" 15th September and 1st May.
6b. Bantry,	Mizen Head to Crow Head.	" 30th September and 1st May.
6c. Kenmare,	Crow Head to Lamb Head.	" 15th September and 1st April.
7. Killarney,	Lamb Head to Dunmore Head, including Blaskets.	" 31st July and 16th January, save Rivers Maine, Ferta, or Valentia, Inny, and Waterville, and their Tributaries. Maine, Ferta or Valentia, Inny, and Tributaries, between 15th September and 1st May. Waterville and its Tributaries, between 16th July and 1st January.
8. Limerick,	Dunmore to Hags Head.	Between 31st July and 12th February, save River Cashen and Tributaries, and save between Kerry Head and Dunmore Head, and between Loop Head and Hags Head, and all Rivers running into the sea between those points. For River Cashen down to its Mouth and Tributaries, between 31st August and 1st June. Between Dunmore Head and Kerry Head, and all Rivers flowing into sea between those points, between 15th September and 1st April. Between Loop Head and Hags Head, and all Rivers running into the sea between those points, between 15th September and 1st May.
9. Galway,	Hags Head to Slyne Head.	Between 15th August and 1st February.
10a. Ballinakill,	Slyne Head to Pigeon Point.	Between the 31st of August and 16th of February, save in Louisburgh and Carrowniskey Rivers and Estuaries. For Louisburgh and Carrowniskey Rivers and Estuaries, between 15th of September and 1st July.
10b. Bangor,	Pigeon Point to Benwee Head.	Between 31st August and 16th February, save in Newport and Glenamoy, Burrishoole and Owengarve Rivers and Estuaries. For Newport River and Estuary, 31st August and 20th March; Glenamoy River and Estuary, 15th September and 1st May; Burrishoole and Owengarve River and Estuaries, 31st August and 16th February.
11. Ballina,	Benwee to Coonamore.	Between 12th August and 16th March, save Palmerstown and Easkey Rivers, which is between 31st August and 1st June.
12. Sligo,	Coonamore to Mullaghmore.	" 19th August and 4th February, save Sligo River, its Estuary and Tributaries, which is between 31st July and 16th January.
13. Ballyshannon,	Mullaghmore to Rossan.	" 19th August and 1st March, save River Eske and Tributaries, which is between 17th September and 1st April.
14. Letterkenny,	Rossan to Malin Head.	" 19th August and 4th Feb., and one mile above Tideway, save Crana or Bunerana, and Gweebarra River. For Crana or Bunerana River, between 14th September and 15th April; for Gweebarra, between 30th Sept. and 1st April.
15a. Londonderry,	Malin to Downhill Boundary.	Between 31st August and 15th April.
15b. Coleraine,	Downhill Boundary to Portrush.	" 19th August and 4th February.
16. Ballycastle,	Portrush to Donaghadee.	" Do. do.
17a. Drogheda,	Skerries to Clogher Head.	" 4th August and 12th February.
17b. Dundalk,	Clogher Head to Donaghadee.	" 31st August and 1st April, save in Annagassan, Glyde, Dee, and Fane Rivers. In Glyde, Dee, and Annagassan Rivers, between 19th August and 12th February; in Fane River between 19th August and 1st April.

NOTE.—The 31st section of the 26th & 27th Vic., c. 114, requires there shall not be fewer than 168 days Close Season in each Fishery.

WEEKLY CLOSE SEASON.—By the 20th section of the 26th & 27th Vic., c. 114 no Salmon or Trout shall be fished for or taken in any way, except by Single Rod and Line, between six of the clock on Saturday morning and six of the clock on the succeeding Monday morning.

No. 17.

the different Districts in Ireland on 31st December, 1878.

No.	Fresh Water.	Angling with Cross Lines.	Angling with Single Rod and Line.	Dates of last change.	Principal Rivers in District. No.
1	Same as Tidal.	Same as Netting.	Between 31st Oct. & 1st day of Feb.	15th Oct. 1874.	1. Liffey, Bray, Vartry.
2	Same as Tidal.	Same as Netting.	Between 30th Sept. and 15th March.	26th Dec. 1878.	2. Slaney, Courtown, Inch, Urrin, Boro.
3	Same as Tidal.	Same as Netting.	Between 30th Sept. and 1st Feb.	12th Nov. 1874.	3. Suir, Nore, and Barrow.
4	Same as Tidal.	Same as Netting.	Between 15th Oct. and 15th Feb.	16th Dec. 1875.	4. Blackwater.
5	Same as Tidal.	Same as Netting.	Between 12th Oct. and 15th of Feb.	28th Dec. 1874.	5. Lee, Bandon, Argideen.
6¹	Between 31st July and 1st May.	Same as Netting.	Between 31st Oct. and 17th March.	30th June, 1870.	6¹. Ilen.
6²	Same as Tidal.	Same as Netting.	Do. do.	29th Jan., 1873.	6². Glengariff, Sneeve, &c.
6³	Same as Tidal.	Between 15th October and 1st April.	Between 31st Oct. and 1st day of Feb.	7th Feb. 1856.	6³. Blackwater, Roughty, Cloonee, Sneem.
7	Same as Tidal.	Same as Netting.	Between 30th Sept. and 1st Feb., save in Maine, Laune, Carra, and Tributaries. Maine and Tributaries, between 30th Sept. and 11th April. Laune, Carra, and Tributaries, between 30th Sept. and 16th Jan.	26th April, 1870. 11th Dec. 1875. 3rd Jan. 1876.	7. Inny, Roughty, Currane, Valencia, Maine, Laune, Carra.
8	Same as Tidal.*	Same as Netting.	Between 30th Sept. and 1st Feb., save Feale, Geale, Cashen, and Maigue Rivers and tributaries and save in all rivers running into the sea, between Loop Head and Hags Head, and between Dunmore Head and Kerry Head. For Feale, Geale, and Cashen and tributaries, between 31st Oct. and 16th March; for Maigue and tributaries, between 30th Sept. and 28th Feb., between Loop Head and Hags Head, between 30th Sept. and 1st March, and between Dunmore Head and Kerry Head, between 30th Sept. and 1st April.	13th Oct. 1874. 17th Sept. 1878.	8. Shannon, Deel, Fergus, Doonbeg, Cashen, Maigue, &c.
9	Same as Tidal.	Same as Netting.	Between 15th Oct. and 1st Feb., save in Cashla, Doohulla, Spiddal, Ballynahinch, Crumlin, Screeb, and Inver Rivers and their lakes and tributaries, which is between 31st Oct. and 1st Feb.	26th Dec. 1871. 23rd Oct. 1875. 17th Sept. 1877. 29th Aug. 1878.	9. Corrib, Cashla, Doohulla, Spiddle, Ballinahinch.
10¹	Same as Tidal.	Same as Netting.	Between 31st Oct. and 1st Feb., save in Louisburgh and Carrowniskey Rivers—between 31st Oct. and 1st July.	1st June, 1872.	10¹. Erriff, Dawros, Louisburgh, Carrowniskey.
10²	Same as Tidal.	Same as Netting.	Between 30th Sept. and 1st May, save in Owenmore and Munhin, which is between 30th Sept. and 1st Feb., and save in Burrishoole, between 31st Oct. and 1st Feb., and save Owengarve and Glenamoy, between 31st Oct. and 1st May, and save Owenduff or Ballycroy, and Ballyveeny and Owenduff, and all rivers in Achill Island, between 31st Oct. and 1st Feb.	1st June, 1872. 7th Oct. 1875. 5th Dec. 1878. Do.	10². Newport, Owenmore, Burrishoole, Owengarve, Glenamoy, Ballyveeny.
11	Between 31st July and 1st Feb., save Palmerston and Easkey Rivers, which is between 31st August and 1st June.	Same as Netting in fresh water.	Between 30th Sept. and 1st Feb., save Easkey River and Tributaries, which is between 30th Sept. and 1st June, and save Cloonaghmore or Palmerston River and Tributaries—tidal, between 31st Oct. and 1st Feb., upper, between 31st Oct. and 1st June.	19th Dec., 1878. 10th July, 1877.	11. Moy, Easkey, Cloonaghmore.
12	Between 19th August and 4th February, save Sligo River, which is between 31st July and 16th January.	Same as Netting in fresh water.	30th Sept. and 1st Feb., save in Drumcliffe River and Glencar Lake between 19th Oct. and 1st Feb.	24th April, 1871. 27th Sept., 1877.	12. Sligo, Ballisodare, Drumcliffe.
13	Same as Tidal.	Same as Netting.	Between 9th Oct. and 1st March, save Bunduff, Bundrowes, and Erne Rivers, and Tributaries, Bunduff River, 30th Sept. and 1st Feb.; Bundrowes, 30th Sept. and 1st Jan., and Erne River, 30th Sept. and 1st March.	24th Nov. 1871. 26th June, 1875.	13. Glen, Inver, Eske, Bunduff, Bundrowes, Erne.
14	Between 19th Aug. and 1st Mar. Crana or Buncrana River, Lennan and Gweebarra Rivers, same as Tidal.	Same as Netting.	Between 1st Nov. and 1st Feb., save in Crana or Buncrana, between 31st Oct. and 1st March.	2nd Sept. 1857. 28th Feb. 1874. 28th Nov. 1874. 21st Mar. 1876.	14. Lennan, Gweedore, Gweebarra, Buncrana.
15¹	Same as Tidal.	28th Sept. and 15th April.	Between 15th Oct. and 1st Mar.	27th Jan. 1862. 19th July, 1877.	15¹. Foyle, Roe.
15²	19th August and 1st March.	28th Sept. & 16th March.†	Between 19th Oct. and 16th Mar., save Rivers Bann, Maine, Sixmilewater, Moyola and Ballinderry, between 31st Oct. and 1st Mar.	18th Dec. 1856. 31st Mar. 1871. 23rd Aug. 1875. 15th Jan. 1876.	15². Bann.
16	Do.	28th Sept. and 16th March.	1st Nov. and 1st Feb.	18th Dec. 1856.	16. Ballycastle, Glenarm, Bush, Glendun.
17¹	Same as Tidal.	Same as Netting.	4th August and 12th Feb.	28th Dec. 1878.	17¹. Boyne.
17²	Same as Tidal.	Same as Netting.	Between 11th Oct. and 1st March, save in Annagassan, Glyde, and Dee Rivers. In Annagassan, Glyde, and Dee Rivers, between 30th Sept. and 1st Feb.	8th July, 1872. 15th Jan. 1876.	17². Fane, Annagassan, Glyde, Dee.

* Close Season for Fixed Engines for the capture of Eels, between the 10th January and 1st July, save in the River Shannon, which is between the 31st January and 1st July, and in all other rivers in the Limerick District between 31st December and 1st July in year following, and save in Drogheda District, which is between 30th November and 1st July, and save in the Coleraine District, which is between 10th January and 1st June, in year following.

† Pollen Fishing by Trammel Nets in Lough Neagh, between 31st October and 1st February.

APPENDIX,

CERTIFICATES granted up to 31st December, 1878, for Fixed Engines for

No.	Place.	Name of Person to whom Certificate granted.	Date of Certificate.	District in which Net erected.	Description of Fixed Net.
65	River Moy,	Mary Anne Little and Andrew Clarke,	2 May, 1870,	Ballina,	6 Fixed draft nets,
67	Ditto,	J. W. Stratford,	18 May, 1870,	Ditto,	2 Ditto,
85	Sea off coast, co. Mayo,	William Little,	8 June, 1870,	Ditto,	2 Bag nets,
109	Sea off coast, co. Sligo,	William Little,	16 May, 1872,	Ditto,	3 Ditto,
2	Sea off co. Antrim,	A. G. Fullerton,	5 September, 1865,	Ballycastle,	1 Ditto,
3	Ditto,	Ditto,	Ditto,	Ditto,	1 Ditto,
5	Ditto,	Thomas Black,	2 October, 1865,	Ditto,	1 Ditto,
6	Ditto,	Ditto,	Ditto,	Ditto,	1 Ditto,
7	Ditto,	Sir E. MacNaghten,	Ditto,	Ditto,	1 Ditto,
8	Ditto,	Thomas Black,	Ditto,	Ditto,	1 Ditto,
9	Ditto,	Earl of Antrim,	22 November 1865,	Ditto,	1 Ditto,
10	Ditto,	Thomas Black,	2 October, 1865,	Ditto,	1 Ditto,
11	Ditto,	Ditto,	21 October, 1865,	Ditto,	1 Ditto,
14	Ditto,	J. C. Anderson,	28 October, 1865,	Ditto,	1 Ditto
15	Ditto,	Ditto,	Ditto,	Ditto,	1 Ditto,
50	Ovalough Bay,	Earl of Antrim,	8 February, 1870,	Ditto,	1 Ditto,
59	Off coast, co. Antrim,	Sir E. W. Macnaghten, bart.,	2 May, 1870,	Ditto,	1 Ditto,
60	Ditto,	Ditto,	Ditto,	Ditto,	1 Ditto,
61	Ditto,	Ditto,	Ditto,	Ditto,	1 Fixed draft net,
66	Ballycastle Bay,	Sir H. H. Boyd, bart.,	Ditto,	Ditto,	1 Ditto,
*70	Sea off coast, co. Antrim,	Denis Black,	12 May, 1870,	Ditto,	1 Ditto,
71	Ditto,	John Finlay,	Ditto,	Ditto,	1 Ditto,
72	Ditto,	John M'Gildowney,	Ditto,	Ditto,	1 Ditto,
73	Ditto,	Edmund M'Neill,	Ditto,	Ditto,	1 Ditto,
74	Red Bay,	H. H. M'Neill,	Ditto,	Ditto,	1 Ditto,
75	Sea off coast, co. Antrim,	Earl of Antrim,	Ditto,	Ditto,	1 Ditto,
82	Ditto,	Lady Boyd, on behalf of Sir H. H. Boyd, bart.	Ditto,	Ditto,	1 Ditto,
84	Ditto,	J. E. Leslie,	Ditto,	Ditto,	1 Ditto,
97	Ditto,	Earl of Antrim,	29 April, 1871,	Ditto,	1 Ditto,
108	Ditto,	Denis Black,	19 July, 1871,	Ditto,	1 Ditto,
116	Ditto,	John Finlay,	9 July, 1872,	Ditto,	1 Ditto,
117	Ditto,	Robert Woodside,	10 July, 1872,	Ditto,	1 Ditto,
23	River Ryne,	Alicia Sheil,	20 January, 1866,	Ballyshannon,	1 Stake net,
64	Sea off Coast of Sligo,	Rt. Hon. W. Cowper Temple,	2 May, 1870,	Ditto,	1 Fixed draft net,
76	Sea off coast, co. Donegal,	H. G. Murray Stewart,	18 May, 1870,	Ditto,	2 Ditto,
79	Inver Bay,	William Sinclair,	Ditto,	Ditto,	3 Ditto,
80	Sea off coast, co. Donegal,	Marquis Conyngham,	Ditto,	Ditto,	1 Ditto,
83	Ditto,	Ebenezer Bustard,	Ditto,	Ditto,	1 Ditto,
90	River Erne,	R. L. Moore and others,	7 February, 1871,	Ditto,	2 Ditto,
62	Island of Achill,	Alexander Hector,	2 May, 1870,	Bangor,	1 Bag net,
65	Owenmore River,	William Pettie,	18 May, 1870,	Ditto,	1 Fixed draft net,
69	Owenmore and Ballycroy Rivers,	Helen Little,	19 May, 1870,	Ditto,	7 Ditto,
110	Sea off coast, co. Mayo,	Sir F. A. K. Gore, bart.,	25 May, 1872,	Ditto,	2 Bag nets,
111	Ditto,	William Pike,	1 July, 1872,	Ditto,	2 Ditto,
112	Ditto,	Trustees Achill Mission,	Ditto,	Ditto,	4 Ditto,
113	Ditto,	Ditto,	Ditto,	Ditto,	5 Ditto,
114	Ditto,	Ditto,	Ditto,	Ditto,	3 Ditto,
1	Sea off co. Londonderry,	Henry O'Neill,	31 August, 1865,	Coleraine,	1 Bag Net,
12	Sea off co. Antrim,	Thomas Black,	21 October, 1865,	Ditto,	1 Ditto,
93	Bann River,	The Irish Society,	15 February, 1871,	Ditto,	4 Fixed draft nets.
20	Ringabella Bay,	Samuel Hodder,	7 March, 1867,	Cork,	1 Bag Net,
56	Cork Harbour,	Sampson French,	22 September, 1870,	Ditto,	1 Stake net,
119	Ditto,	John Charles Bennett,	28 December, 1876,	Ditto,	1 Ditto,
13	Sea off co. Louth,	Sir Alan E. Bellingham,	28 October, 1865,	Dundalk,	1 Head Weir,
18	Ditto,	John P. Jones,	16 November, 1865,	Ditto,	1 Bag Net,
115	Ditto,	Arthur Newcomen	10 July, 1872,	Ditto,	1 Ditto,
4	Kenmare River,	R. B. Mahony,	16 January, 1866,	Kenmare,	1 Ditto,
51	River Leannane (Estuary),	Sir J. Stewart, bart.,	13 May, 1870,	Letterkenny,	1 Fixed draft net,
118	Sea off coast, co. Donegal,	Charles F. Stewart,	19 June, 1875,	Ditto,	3 Bag nets,
121	Estuary of Crana or Castle River,	Alexander A. Richardson,	8 October, 1877,	Ditto,	1 Fixed draft net,
17	River Shannon,	William B. Barrington,	7 November, 1865,	Limerick,	1 Fly Net,
24	Ditto,	S. Cunningham,	16 March, 1866,	Ditto,	1 Stake Net,
25	River Banratty,	Thomas Studdert,	11 February, 1867.	Ditto,	1 Head Weir,
31	Doonmore Strand,	John Scott,	19 May, 1868,	Ditto,	1 Salmon Weir or Wall.
32	Doonbeg Strand,	W. Simpeale,	Ditto,	Ditto,	1 Ditto,
35	Shannon,	William Creagh Hickie,	8 February, 1870,	Ditto,	1 Stake net,
36	Ditto,	Colonel C. M. Vandeleur,	Ditto,	Ditto	1 Ditto,
37	Clonderalaw Bay,	Lord Annaly,	Ditto,	Ditto,	1 Ditto,
38	Ditto,	Ditto,	Ditto,	Ditto,	1 Ditto,
39	Ditto,	Ditto,	Ditto,	Ditto,	1 Ditto,
40	Ditto,	R. W. C. Reeves,	Ditto,	Ditto,	1 Ditto,
41	Ditto,	Ditto,	Ditto,	Ditto,	1 Ditto,
42	Ditto,	Ditto,	Ditto,	Ditto,	1 Ditto,
43	Ditto,	Ditto,	Ditto,	Ditto,	1 Ditto,
44	Shannon,	Knight of Glin,	Ditto,	Ditto,	1 Ditto,
45	Ditto,	G. H. Minchin,	Ditto,	Ditto,	1 Ditto,
46	Clonderalaw Bay,	Col. H. Hickman,	Ditto,	Ditto,	1 Ditto,
49	Shannon,	John Griffin,	Ditto,	Ditto,	1 Ditto,
52	Ditto,	Leslie Wren,	Ditto,	Ditto,	1 Ditto,
53	Ditto,	Ditto,	Ditto,	Ditto,	1 Ditto,

* This certificate lapsed.

No. 18.

fishing for Salmon or Trout (arranged in Districts).

No.	Particulars of Size, &c.	Observations
65	6 nets, from 150 to 250 yards in length,	—
67	3 nets, not exceeding 60 yards in length,	Sourmore fixed nets.
85	Leaders, 58 fathoms long each; and each bag about 7 feet wide,	Kilcummin bag nets.
109	Leaders, each 50 fathoms long; heads, 6 fathoms each,	Enniscrone nets.
2	Leader, 73 yards; net, 28 yards,	Larrybane net.
3	Leader, 34 yards; net, 20 yards,	Carrickarede net.
5	Leader, 600 feet; net, 66 feet,	Cusman net.
6	Leader, 330 feet; net, 66 feet,	Big Duncan net.
7	Leader, 240 feet; net, 84 feet,	Portbraddan net.
8	Leader, 240 feet; net, 66 feet,	Skarryvan net.
9	Leader, 150 feet; net, 40 feet,	Torr net.
10	Leader, 240 feet; net, 66 feet,	Little Dunseverick net.
11	Leader, 280 feet; net, 60 feet,	Portnean net.
14	Net, 110 feet; head, 63 feet,	Portfad net.
15	Ditto ditto,	Portmoon net.
58	Leader, 115 yards long; head 43 feet long,	Carnlough net.
59	Leader, 75 yards long; head, 21 yards long,	Blackrock bag net.
60	Leader, 74 yards long; head, 21 yards long,	Glashan Island bag net.
61	Length, 100 yards,	Croggenagh net.
69	Length, 100 yards,	Ballycastle net.
70	Length, 300 feet,	Moneyvart fixed draft net.
71	Length, 80 yards,	Ballyleerim fixed net.
72	Length, 104 yards,	Clerapark fixed net.
73	Length, 90 yards,	Currysheskin fixed net.
74	Length, 110 yards,	Red Bay fixed draft net.
75	Length, 108 yards,	Loyd fixed draft net.
83	Length, 90 yards,	Kinbane net.
84	Length, 75 yards,	Templastragh net.
97	120 yards long,	Pier net.
108	Length, 100 yards,	Moneyvart, otherwise Portvinegar, draft net.
116	43 fathoms long,	Stame net.
117	Leader, 74 yards long; head, 26 yards long,	Craggaboy net.
28	Land arm, 210 yards fixed,	Erne weir.
64	Length, 120 yards long,	Mullaghmore net.
78	2 nets, not exceeding 150 yards in length,	Mockrosh Gortalla nets.
79	2 nets, 140 yards long,	Inver nets.
80	Length, 120 yards,	Ballyederlane net.
83	Length, 90 yards,	Drumbarna net.
90	Each 200 yards long,	—
62	Leader, 100 yards long; head, 18 yards long,	Keel net.
68	4 nets, not exceeding 180 yards in length,	Owenmore nets.
69	7 Ditto, 300 ditto,	Tullaghan nets.
110	Leaders, 40 fathoms long; heads, 5 fathoms long,	Cashleeha and Doogbeg nets.
111	Leaders, 40 fathoms long, and heads 5 fathoms long,	Dooega nets.
112	Leaders, 40 fathoms; heads, 5 fathoms long,	Slievemore nets.
113	Leader, 40 fathoms long; head, 5 fathoms long,	Dooport nets.
114	Ditto, ditto,	Keel nets.
3	Net, 130 yards—first pole from shore, 12 yards; last do., 130 yards,	Ballygelagh net.
12	Leader, 324 feet; net, 66 feet,	Flagstaff net.
86	Not exceeding 240 yards length,	—
26	Leader, 240 feet; length of net, 22 feet,	Ringabella net.
86	Length, 90 yards,	Conkinny net.
119	Length, 158 feet—such measurement not to extend said fixed engine beyond the low water mark of ordinary spring tides.	Bennett's Court stake net.
15	South side, 627 feet; east side, 204½ feet; Fish Pass south side, 3½ feet; open at end in river, 4½ feet,	Castlebellingham weir.
18	Leader, 300 feet; bag, 42 feet; first pole, 300 feet from fixed point on shore,	Drogheda town net.
115	Leader, 50 fathoms long; head, 9 fathoms,	St. Dennis's Well net.
4	Leader, 240 feet; net, 54 feet,	Bath.
81	Length, 120 yards,	Leenane net.
118	Leaders not exceeding 80 yards each in length, and the heads 24 yards in length and 10 yards in width.	Horn Head nets.
121	Length not exceeding 85 yards,	Orana fixed net.
17	Weir, 190 feet; H.W.M. to in-pole, 90 feet,	Shannon Lawn weir.
24	Wing, 42 yards; ebb wing, 46 yards,	Aylevaroo weir.
25	138 feet; 18 feet eye,	Bunratty weir.
31	600 feet,	Dunmore weir.
33	1,284 feet,	Dernabeg weir.
35	308 yards long,	Cloonamon weir.
36	The leader, 274 feet long; and head, 30 feet long and 19 feet wide,	Mount Shannon weir.
37	The first or shore leader 167 yards long, the head 20 yards long and 14½ yards wide. The second leader 136 yards long; and the second head 20 yards long and 14½ yards wide.	Millpark weir.
38	The first or shore leader, 134 yards long; first head, 20 yards long and 14½ yards wide. The second leader, 180 yards long; second head, 20 yards long and 14½ yards wide.	Lackanabehee weir.
39	The leader 120 yards long, and the head 20 yards long by 14½ yards wide,	Lahyle weir.
40	The leader 60 yards long, and the head 23 yards long and 7 yards wide,	Lynch's Point weir.
41	The leader 115 yards long, and the head 23 yards long and 12 yards wide,	Park Rough weir.
42	The leader 78 yards long, and the head 28 yards long and 9 yards wide,	Poulnagullky weir.
43	The leader 80 yards long, and the head 28 yards long and 11 yards wid	Woodpoint weir.
44	The first leader 493 feet long; first head 45½ feet. Second leader, 234 feet long; second head, 73½ feet. Third leader, 243 feet long; third head, 73 feet; and the fourth leader, 272½ feet long; fourth head, 73 feet.	Long Rock weir.
45	Leader, 49½ yards long; and head, 22 yards long,	Killaoolla weir.
48	The first leader, 169 yards long; first head, 14 yards long. Second leader, 111 yards long; second head, 34 yards long.	Kilmore Point weir.
49	The first leader, 231 feet long; first head, 39 feet long and 13 feet wide. Second leader, 223 feet long; second head, 73 feet long and 16½ feet wide. Third leader, 183 feet long; head, 37 feet long and 17 feet wide.	Carrowbanaheg weir.
52	Entire length, 324 yards,	Carrigane weir.
53	Entire length, 167 yards,	Kylanillin weir.

Appendix, No. 18.

Certificates for Fixed Engines.

APPENDIX,

CERTIFICATES granted up to 31st December, 1878, for Fixed

No.	Place.	Name of Person to whom Certificate granted.	Date of Certificate.	District in which Net situated.	Description of Fixed Net.
54	Shannon,	Baron Monteagle,	11 February, 1870,	Limerick,	1 Stake Net,
55	Ditto,	Ditto,	Ditto,	Ditto,	1 Ditto,
56	Ditto,	Ditto,	Ditto,	Ditto,	1 Ditto,
57	Ditto,	Ditto,	Ditto,	Ditto,	1 Ditto,
86	Ditto,	Thomas Sanders,	12 March, 1870,	Ditto,	1 Ditto,
87	Ditto,	Robert Leslie,	16 January, 1871,	Ditto,	1 Ditto,
88	Ditto,	Ditto,	Ditto,	Ditto,	1 Ditto,
89	Ditto,	Thomas Sandes,	Ditto,	Ditto,	1 Ditto,
101	Ditto,	Lord Annaly,	18 November, 1871,	Ditto,	1 Ditto,
102	Ditto,	Ditto,	Ditto,	Ditto,	1 Ditto,
103	Ditto,	R. W. C. Reeves,	11 November, 1871,	Ditto,	1 Ditto,
104	Ditto,	Colonel Vandeleur,	18 November, 1871,	Ditto,	1 Ditto,
105	Ditto,	Ditto,	11 November, 1871,	Ditto,	2 Ditto,
106	Ditto,	Ditto,	18 November, 1871,	Ditto,	1 Ditto,
107	Ditto,	Bonamon Cox,	11 November, 1871,	Ditto,	1 Ditto,
120	Ditto,	Daniel Borough,	19 May, 1877,	Ditto,	1 Ditto,
122	Ditto,	Robert Leslie,	24 April, 1878,	Ditto,	2 Ditto,
124	Shannon, off Scattery Island,	Marcus Keane,	31 January, 1879,	Ditto,	8 Ditto,
123	Shannon,	William Creagh Hickie,	Ditto,	Ditto,	1 Ditto,
125	Shannon, off Carrig Island,	Charles Sandes,	7 March, 1879,	Ditto,	1 Ditto,
16	Ballycotton Bay,	John Iston,	31 October, 1863,	Lismore,	1 Bag Net,
28	River Blackwater,	John Neill and William Hennessy,	14 January, 1864,	Ditto,	1 Stake Net,
98	Ditto,	Trustees, Provincial Bank,	13 February, 1873,	Ditto,	1 Stake Weir,
99	Ditto,	Hon. C. W. Moore Smyth,	21 June, 1871,	Ditto,	1 Ditto,
20	Lough Foyle,	The Irish Society,	2 January, 1866,	Londonderry,	1 Stake Net,
21	Ditto,	Ditto,	Ditto,	Ditto,	1 Ditto,
22	Ditto,	Ditto,	Ditto,	Ditto,	1 Ditto,
30	Sea off co. Donegal,	George Young,	27 April, 1868,	Ditto,	1 Bag Net,
33	Ditto,	Ditto,	6 October, 1869,	Ditto,	1 Ditto,
34	Ditto,	Ditto,	Ditto,	Ditto,	1 Ditto,
63	Magilligan Strand,	Sir H. H. Bruce, bart.,	2 May, 1870,	Ditto,	1 Ditto,
76	Sea off coast, co. Londonderry,	Alexander Shalders, A. W. White, and R. J. Broughton	11 May, 1870,	Ditto,	4 Fixed draft nets,
77	Ditto,	John Cromie,	Ditto,	Ditto,	3 Ditto,
93	Magilligan Strand,	Sir H. Bruce, bart.,	22 April, 1871,	Ditto,	1 Ditto,
94	Ditto,	James M'Gowery,	15 February, 1871,	Ditto,	1 Ditto,
95	Ditto,	William Lorion,	Ditto,	Ditto,	1 Ditto,
96	River Foyle,	The Irish Society,	Ditto,	Ditto,	8 Ditto,
27	Sea off co. Sligo,	Ormsby Jones,	4 November, 1867,	Sligo,	1 Bag Net,
29	Ditto,	Lady Palmerston and Right Hon. W. Cowper-Temple,	20 January, 1868,	Ditto,	1 Ditto,
91	Sligo River,	Abraham Martin,	20 February, 1871,	Ditto,	2 Fixed draft nets,
108	Drumcliffe River,	William Petrie,	12 April, 1871,	Ditto,	1 Ditto,
19	Barrow, otherwise Suir, Nore, and Barrow conjoined,	Lord Templemore,	4 December, 1863,	Waterford,	1 Head Weir,
46	Waterford Harbour,	A. N. O'Neill,	8 February, 1870,	Ditto,	1 Stake Net,
47	Ditto,	Ditto,	Ditto,	Ditto,	1 Ditto,
51	King's Channel,	Ditto,	Ditto,	Ditto,	2 Ditto,

Appendix, No. 19.

APPENDIX,

RESULT of INQUIRIES held by the INSPECTORS of IRISH FISHERIES into the Legality or Illegality of

No.	Where Fixed Net situated.	Description of Fixed Net	Name of Person maintaining and using Fixed Net.	Name of Owner of Fixed Net, or of Land to which Net attached.	Name of Townland to which Net attached.	Parish.
400	River Shannon,	1 Stake net,	Margaret Borough,	Margaret Borough,	Querrin,	Moyarta,
401	Do.,	2 Do.	Robert Leslie,	Robert Leslie,	Kilpaddoge,	Kilnaughtin,
402	River Shannon, off Scattery Island,	4 Do.	Marcus Keane,	Marcus Keane,	Scattery Island,	Kilrush,
403	River Shannon,	1 Do.,	William C. Hickie,	William C. Hickie,	Clonderalaw,	Aghavallen,
404	Do.,	1 Do.,	Charles Sandes,	Charles Sandes,	Carrig Island,	Do.,
405	Do.,	1 Do.,	Do.,	Do.,	Do.,	Do.,

Appendix No. 20.

APPENDIX, No. 20.

QUANTITY of SALMON exported to undermentioned places in England, from Ireland, from 1st January to 31st December, 1878.

	No. of Boxes of 130 lbs each	
London,	4,378	computed at 1s. 3d. per lb. Value delivered at foregoing places would be £418,476 11s 3d
Nottingham,	2,793	
Bradford,	3,679	
Manchester,	6,555	
Sheffield,	4,641	
Wolverhampton,	3,110	
Leeds,	4,000½	
Liverpool,	8,761	
Birmingham,	6,720	
Total, 1878,	44,637½	
Total, 1877,	47,934 : Decrease,	3,296½

APPENDIX, No. 18.

Certificates for fixed Engines.

No. 18—*continued.*

Engines for fishing for Salmon or Trout—*continued.*

No.	Particulars of Size, &c.	Observations.
84	Leader, 280 feet long, head, 84 feet long.	Foyne's Island (south) weir.
85	Leader, 187 feet long; head, 80 feet long, and 18 feet 6 inches wide,	Foyne's Island (north) weir.
86	The first leader, 398 feet long; first head 103 feet long and 14 feet wide. Second leader, 228 feet long; second head, 96 feet long and 13 feet wide.	Durnish weir.
87	The first leader, 300 feet long; first head, 40 feet long and 33 feet wide. Second leader, 210 feet long; second head, 98 feet long. 13 feet wide.	Mount Trenchard weir.
88	Size—327 feet from high-water mark.	Coolanoonagh weir.
97	Length, 117 yards.	Tarbert net.
98	Length, 67 yards.	Kilpadogue net.
99	Length, 92 yards 2 feet,	Ballyspara net.
101	Leader, 110 yards long.	River weir.
102	Leader, 70 yards long.	Beetory weir.
103	Leader, 165 yards long; head, 26 yards, and 8 wide.	Poulnadarree weir
104	Leader, 69 yards long; head, 7 yards long.	Ayelvarree or Ballynote west weir
105	E. Weir, leader, 78 yards long; head, 17 yards—W. Weir leader, 25 yards long; 2 heads each, 17 yards long	Carrowdotia eastern & western weirs.
106	Leader, 90 yards long; head, 17 yards long.	Colmanstown weir.
107	5 leaders, each 120 yards, and 3 heads, each 17 yards long,	Clarefield weir.
120	4 heads, whole length not to exceed 550 yards, measurements not to extend fixed engine below low water of ordinary spring tides	Shanganagh weir.
122	No. 1, 112 yards in length, and No. 2, 90 yards in length, measurements not to extend fixed engines below low water of ordinary spring tides.	—
124	C net, 800 yards long; D net, 138 yards long; and E net, 325 yards long.	Scattery Island weirs.
123	Three heads; the whole length not exceeding 350 yards.	Cloonarran weir.
125	200 yards long.	Carrig Island weir.
16	271 feet,	Ballyeatten net.
28	125 feet, Leader,	Scart weir.
86	Length of Shore-arm, 70 feet; body of Weir, 88 feet; Flood-arm, 13 feet; large yard, width, 18 feet; Fish pocket, width, 17 feet.	Stuel weir.
29	Leader, 84 feet long; head, 106 feet—Ballinatray Weir.	Ballynatray weir.
30	In-pole of Shore Leader to outer pole of same, 155 feet; out-pole of do. to do. of Ebb Leader, 82 feet; out-pole of chambers of net channelwards, 17 feet.	The Creek weir.
31	In-pole of Shore Leader to outer pole of same, 196 feet; out-pole of do. to do. of Flood Leader, 112 feet; out-pole of chambers of net channelwards, 22 feet.	The Shell Rock weir.
32	In-pole of Shore Leader to outer pole of same, 262 feet; out-pole of do. to do. of Flood Leader, 192 feet,	The Chapel Brook weir.
30	348 feet, inner to outer pole,	Cloggus net.
33	Leader, 270 feet; bag, 75 feet,	Bunagaun net.
34	Ditto, ditto,	Carrickafoal net.
65	Leader, 318 yards long; head, 17 yards long.	Ballymaclary net.
74	2—220 yards in length; and 2—140 yards in length,	Cromragh and Tullaghearney nets
77	2 nets, 180 yards long, and 1—122 yards long,	Mullaghmeal nets.
82	Not exceeding 240 yards length,	—
84	160 yards long,	—
86	150 yards long.	—
85	From 100 to 200 yards long,	—
87	Leader, 110 yards; length of net, 20 yards,	Streedagh net.
89	566 feet, inner to outer pole,	Mullaghmore net.
91	Each net exceeding 135 yards length,	—
106	180 yards in length,	Drumcliffe net.
19	Shore wing, 235 feet; channel wing, 94 feet; space between shore wing and rock, 45 feet,	Ballinasmall Castle weir.
46	The first leader, 283 yards long; and the second leader, 426 yards 1 foot long,	Knockaveelish weir.
47	The first leader, 452 yards long; second leader, 398 yards 1 foot long,	Woodstown weir
51	Lower weir—leader, 88 yards long; upper weir—leader, 33 yards long. The head or pocket of the former extending from west to east 34 yards in breadth, and the latter extending from west to east 52 yards.	King's Channel weirs (2).

No. 19.

APPENDIX, No. 19.

Fixed Nets erected or used for catching Salmon in Ireland, during the year 1878, and to 31st March, 1879.

No.	Barony.	County.	Judgment of Commissioners.	Date of Judgment.	Whether Judgment of Commissioners appealed against.	Result of Appeal in Court of Queen's Bench.
400	Moyarta,	Clare,	Refused,	23rd March, 1878.	Appeal.	—
401	Iraghticonnor,	Kerry,	Legal,	Do.	—	—
402	Moyarta,	Clare,	Report made to Court,	—	—	Judgment reversed.
403	Iraghticonnor,	Kerry,	Legal,	8th January, 1879.	—	—
404	Do.	Do.,	Adjourned,	—	—	—
405	Do.	Do.,	Legal,	29th January, 1879.	—	—

APPENDIX, No. 21.

APPENDIX, No. 21.

QUANTITY of SALMON consigned to Billingsgate Market, from Ireland, during the year 1878.

4,378 large boxes, average weight 150 lbs. each, at 1s. 3d. per lb., equal to £41,043 15s. 0d.

www.ingramcontent.com/pod-product-compliance
Lightning Source LLC
Chambersburg PA
CBHW020235090426
42735CB00010B/1702

* 9 7 8 3 7 4 1 1 0 4 5 3 4 *